Rodin Graphics

Cover: *Antonin Proust*, state 4 (see Fig. 59).

Portrait of Auguste Rodin by Alphonse Legros. c. 1885–1890. Etching.
9-13/16 x 6⅞ in. (24.9 x 17.5 cm.). Bibliothèque Nationale.

Rodin Graphics:
A Catalogue Raisonné of Drypoints and Book Illustrations

by Victoria Thorson

The Fine Arts Museums of San Francisco

Published on the occasion
of an exhibition
at the California Palace
of the Legion of Honor
14 June through 10 August 1975

*This publication is supported
by a grant from the National
Endowment for the Arts in
Washington, D.C., a Federal agency.*

*Copyright © 1975
by The Fine Arts Museums of San Francisco*
ISBN *0-88401-007-4*
Library of Congress Catalogue No. 75-16941

Managing Editor: *F. Lanier Graham*
Editor: *Ann Karlstrom*

Design & Production: *Jack W. Stauffacher
of the Greenwood Press, San Francisco
Text set in Bembo types; display Hunt Roman type.
Type composition by Peters Typesetting, Inc.
Lithography by Reliable, Inc., San Francisco*

Contents

Preface

The San Francisco Bay Area has become the most important center for Rodin studies outside Paris. The extremely rich collection that Mrs. Spreckels gave to the California Palace of the Legion of Honor is now complemented by the gift of the very important collection of Mr. B. Gerald Cantor to Stanford University. Under the guidance of Professor Albert Elsen at Stanford and Professor Jacques de Caso at the University of California at Berkeley, much important work on Rodin is being done by numerous scholars.

It is a privilege and a pleasure for The Fine Arts Museums of San Francisco to participate in the growing understanding of this artist, whom Dr. Thorson properly describes as "the greatest sculptor since Michelangelo."

Ian McKibbin White
Director of Museums

Acknowledgments

The preparation and publication of this catalogue raisonné has been done under the sponsorship and encouragement of The Fine Arts Museums of San Francisco with the help of financial subsidies from the City and County of San Francisco and the National Endowment for the Arts. To these several bodies, I wish to extend my appreciation.

I also am greatly indebted to Ian McKibbin White, Director, F. Lanier Graham, William H. Elsner, Thomas H. Garver, E. Gunter Troche, Fenton Kastner and S. DeRenne Coerr of The Fine Arts Museums of San Francisco for their aid in the conception and organization of the exhibition over the last four years.

The main contributor to the exhibition is the Musée Rodin in Paris, where the Conservateur, Monique Laurent, and the Conservateur Adjoint, Claudie Judrin, have been most generous in their loan of works and in making it possible for me to see nearly all of the over 7,000 Rodin drawings and numerous folders of Rodin's correspondence.

I would also like to acknowledge the important contribution of many other museums and private collectors, whose names appear in the catalogue, for their loan of works and assistance in providing information and photographs. I am grateful as well for the help of Michel Melot and Gisele Lambert at the Bibliothèque Nationale, Cabinet des Estampes, Genevieve Monnier at the Louvre; Joseph Rankin at the Spencer Collection, New York Public Library; Riva Castleman of The Museum of Modern Art in New York; Kneeland McNulty and Starr Behringher at the Philadelphia Museum of Art. I am also indebted to Professor Albert Elsen for his continued encouragement of my Rodin researches and to Kirk Varnedoe for sharing with me his recent thoughts on Rodin's graphic work. Finally, I wish to thank Ann Karlstrom for the editing and Phyllis Hattis, Donna Stein, and Professor Ruth Weisberg for their insightful comments on the manuscript.

Victoria Thorson
Guest Curator

Lenders to the Exhibition

The Art Institute of Chicago
The Baltimore Museum of Art
The Bancroft Library, University of California, Berkeley
Mr. and Mrs. Laurence Brunswick, Jr., Rydal, Pennsylvania
The Cleveland Museum of Art
The Fine Arts Museums of San Francisco
Houghton Library, Harvard University, Cambridge
Kunsthalle Bremen, Bremen, Germany
R. M. Light & Co., Boston
Musée Rodin, Paris
Museum of Fine Arts, Boston
New York Public Library, Astor, Lenox and Tilden Foundations
Stanford University Museum of Art, Stanford

Introduction

Auguste Rodin, the greatest sculptor since Michelangelo, is known to the public primarily for sculptures such as the massive seated figure *The Thinker* and the towering *Balzac*, but he also applied his genius to drypoint printmaking and book illustration. He demonstrated his incredible artistic reserves by quickly mastering the delicate execution and new mental disciplines demanded by these alternative means of expression. Another facet of the sculptor emerges when he is seen as a drypoint engraver, working most actively between 1881 and 1888. With the strength and agility of a mature sculptor he controlled the angle and pressure of the steel needle as he drew lines into a copper plate which furrowed up a metal burr alongside. After the plate was inked and wiped, ink trapped in the metal burrs printed rich lines and velvety black areas unique to drypoint engraving, in contrast to the more even line engraved with a burin or etched with acid. Only drypoint, of all the printmaking media, provided the rich contrast of tone and delicate line which enabled Rodin to create the vibrating profiles and shifting surface planes found in his sculptures. The rich black tonalities and vibrant lights of Rodin's drypoint prints suggest the dark cavities and strong highlights of his bronzes.

In yet another role, as book illustrator, Rodin perused his vast store of drawings to find and rework those corresponding to his thoughts on the four texts he illustrated: *Enguerrande*, by Emile Bergerat, illustrated in 1884; *Les Fleurs du Mal*, by Charles Baudelaire, in 1887–1888; *Le Jardin des Supplices*, by Octave Mirbeau, in 1899; and *Les Elégies amoureuses d'Ovide*, a posthumous publication purportedly illustrated by Rodin c. 1900. For *Enguerrande* and *Les Fleurs du Mal*, Rodin drew in a style paralleling his drypoint technique of the same period. He appears to have sought the same richness of tonality and sculptural volume in his ink drawings for the book illustrations that he had achieved in drypoint with the incised line and the ink spilled by the burr. The ink drawings are either contour drawings elegantly simplified by tracing, which Rodin called *au trait*, or drawings he considered *ombrées*, or shaded. In the *ombrées* drawings Rodin molded the figures and shaded the background with sensitive hachure. In a few drawings for *Les Fleurs du Mal*, he created tonality with layers of black ink highlighted with white gouache.

The tenebrist effects which Rodin sought in many of his illustrations were criticized in his first drawing for *Enguerrande*. Bergerat, speaking for his editor, asked Rodin to eliminate the dark background and to give the figure a more obviously sculptural pose and contour which the public would expect: "It is not necessary to have a black background. It is a drawing of a sculptor not of a painter and the bearing and contour are what is of interest coming from your hand."[1]

Letters such as this one from Bergerat as well as other discoveries recently made at the Musée Rodin in Paris (including a contract between Rodin, Mirbeau, and the publisher Ambroise Vollard for the deluxe edition of *Le Jardin des Supplices* with Rodin's illustrations, as well as preparatory drawings for all of the books) allow an evaluation of the extent of Rodin's collaboration with authors and publishers and his consideration of the texts he illustrated. These documents oppose the prevailing view that Rodin's illustrations merely reproduce drawings in a poetic or literary context, an attitude most commonly taken toward the last two books which he illustrated, *Le Jardin des Supplices* (1899) and *Les Elégies amoureuse d'Ovide* (c.1900).

Rodin's venture into the media of illustration and drypoint came at a time of great ferment in his career as a sculptor. In 1881 he made the decision to abandon his imaginative drawings as a source for the *Gates of Hell*, commissioned the previous year, and to model the clay figures directly from life. That year he also went to England where he stayed with Alphonse Legros, his former schoolmate from the Petite Ecole who was by then a professor of printmaking and well-known painter, sculptor and engraver; there Rodin tried his first drypoint on the back of a plate of Legros. Three years later in 1884, the same year that Rodin received another landmark commission, *The Burghers of Calais*, he collaborated on his first book illustration for Bergerat's *Enguerrande*. By 1900 Rodin had produced twelve drypoints and one lithograph and had illustrated four books, a small but innovative body of work in these two media.

His book illustrations and drypoints are confined to the two decades of his life between 1880 and 1900, the years of his forties and fifties when he was in his prime as an innovator. From 1900 to his death in 1917, Rodin stopped experimenting with these two alternative expressions.[2] In these later years he spent his time creating new portrait busts, supervising a large workshop to reproduce his sculpture, and continuing his lifelong passion of drawing, as he could now afford to draw regularly from the live model.

1. Letter from Emile Bergerat to Rodin, dated July 30, 1884, Musée Rodin archives, Bergerat folder. The entire letter is reproduced in this catalogue under book illustrations: *Enguerrande*.

2. Rodin made only one drypoint after 1900, and it was done in 1916 as a printed acknowledgment of contributions to a war veterans' fund. See discussion of the last drypoint in this catalogue, no. xiii.

Drypoints

Editorial Note

Dimensions are given in inches and centimeters, height preceding width. The dimensions of the drypoints and illustrations may vary a fraction of an inch depending on differences such as paper type. Paper type and collections have been given wherever possible, but this information is by no means exhaustive. Full information for all short references to literature may be found in the Selected Bibliography. In addition, the following two frequently cited volumes are given even shorter references:

Delteil   Delteil, Loys. *Rude, Barye, Carpeaux, Rodin—Le Peintre-graveur illustré XIX et XX siècles.* Vol. 6. Paris: Delteil, 1910.

Grappe   Grappe, Georges. *Catalogue du Musée Rodin.* (All references are to the 1944 edition.)

The Musée Rodin in Paris is listed simply as "Musée Rodin," except in cases where the museum's number is available and the reference becomes MR followed by the number.

Introduction to Drypoints

Rodin's highly prized drypoint portraits of Victor Hugo, Henri Becque and Antonin Proust have been compared to the drypoint portraits of Rembrandt and the style of his drypoint figure compositions to the style of Correggio and Prud'hon. Commenting years later to his most reliable biographer, Judith Cladel, about his success with the new drypoint medium, he said: "I understood it immediately."[1] His ease in mastering drypoint was facilitated by the mature techniques and imagery he had already developed in other media: decoration of vases at the Sèvres Porcelain Manufactory, an unusual "black" drawing style, and a unique method of modeling successive profiles in sculpture.

Between 1879 and 1882 Rodin worked at the Sèvres Manufactory, taking the last of a series of jobs in the decorative arts to support himself as a sculptor. At Sèvres he made designs of bacchants, putti, and other figures in the lyrical mood of Second Empire Neo-Hellenism sobered by his own predilection for strong, truthful emotion. These designs are related thematically to the drypoints *Love Turning the World* (Fig. 1), the upper half of *Figure Studies* (Fig. 5), *Le Printemps* (Fig. 13) and the *Amphora* (Fig. 24), executed between 1881 and 1888, a time which overlaps his Sèvres period.

The style of the earliest drypoints also corresponds to drawings and tracings for Sèvres designs characterized in general by supple contour lines, fine parallel lines and crosshatchings. Rodin's experience with Sèvres techniques also prepared the way for his approach to the new drypoint medium. As observed by a fellow worker, Rodin specially prepared the surface of a standard Sèvres vase form with a thick ceramic paste so that he could cut a deeply incised contour line and then highlight the projections by applying liquid clay with a brush.[2] When cutting a design into the paste, Rodin understood the relation of the incised line to the shadows created by the relief. This experience undoubtedly helped him to grasp the relationship in drypoint between the incised line and the velvety black areas produced by the inked burr. Archive notes at Sèvres and Roger Marx's descriptions from 1900 actually call the incising of a design on a vase *graveur*.[3] In 1899 one biographer observed of Rodin's earlier Sèvres experience, "the craft of an engraver seemed a logical continuation."[4]

Rodin's personal drawing style at the time he took up drypoint was a mature and highly original mode known as his "black" drawing style and would itself have been sufficient to distinguish him as a printmaker. He may have drawn confidence in approaching drypoint essentially as a draftsman from Legros' attitude that "engraving was nothing more than drawing on copper."[5] Of the engraving media, drypoint is the closest to drawing because it is done by drawing directly on the plate with a steel needle, although a strong and skillful hand is required to control the force and angle of the needle. Rodin may also have been encouraged by the attitude prevailing among the connoisseurs of his time, voiced by Roger Marx in 1893, that all graphic media are related: "Whether this drawing be the stroke of a pencil, a pen, a paintbrush on paper, whether it penetrates into the depths of the copper plate, whether it emerges on the surface of the wood, whether it is written on stone . . . little does it matter to us . . . as long as it transmits the force of action of the original thought once it is in print."[6]

The four drypoints which most clearly have their origin in the "black" drawing style are the lower half of *Figure Studies* (Fig. 5), *La Ronde* (Fig. 18), *The Dying Centaur* (Fig. 64), and *Souls of Purgatory* (Fig. 68). This style resulted from Rodin's tracing, reworking or creating new compositions from his drawings of the previous decade or even from his student work (1854–1864). One of the modes continued from the earliest work was a dark, bold contour technique describing active, muscular figures. The contours became stronger when reworked in the 1880's with more continuous lines and often with dramatic black washes, white gouache and sepia tones. Their holocaustic tonality as well as their nightmarish, Dantesque themes prompted the name "black" drawing style. From these drawings, Rodin brought to engraving a personal fantasy imagery, a mature and distinct contour technique and a dramatic sense of "color" or tonality.

Rodin also distinguished himself as a sculptor-engraver because of the unique methods he developed as a sculptor. When modeling a statue or bust, Rodin moved around the figure working successively on the multiple profiles like "a draughtsman outlining in clay the thousand profiles that your head would present if it were sliced a thousand times through the center at different angles."[7] This was the account given by George Bernard Shaw, who sat for a bust by Rodin in 1906 and who also described, tongue in cheek but no doubt with some truth, the experience of turning his head tiny increments while Rodin modeled each profile: "After a while, I was finally so used to turn my head little by little, that I nearly developed a tic."[8] The traditional Beaux-Arts sculptor, by contrast, modeled only from one side and worked from the front surface to the back producing what Rodin felt was a flat relief effect.

Bronze busts were the basis for all of Rodin's drypoint portraits, all of which were executed between 1882 and 1888: *Bust of Bellona* (Fig. 8), *Henri Becque* (Fig. 25), *Victor Hugo, Three-Quarters View* (Fig. 32), *Victor Hugo, Front View* (Fig. 46), and *Antonin Proust* (Fig. 55), and all of which rely on his technique of considering successive profiles in a complete rotation, thus escaping the two-dimensional confines of the copper plate. On all but *Bellona*, the earliest drypoint portrait, Rodin's strokes are never completely parallel nor are they placed at an obvious angle in relation to the flat plane of the plate. Instead they undulate, conforming to the subject's topography, and sensitively graph each tiny fluctuation of the profiles. In *Henri Becque* long, supple, vibrating lines mark profile after profile. In *Antonin Proust* more delicate lines gather in the minute crevices and thin out over the lighter, heightened surfaces. These lines, often blending contour with hachure, create a fine undulating web drawn over the entire skull as Rodin pursued exacting structural accuracy and penetrating characterization.

Rodin first developed his unique hachure technique in a group of drawings carefully copied from his sculptures to illustrate them for Salon catalogues and art periodicals, and he employed the treatment in the drypoint portraits he did from 1883 to 1888. The style was fully developed by 1880 in the drawing after the statue *St. John the Baptist* (Fig. i) and is characterized by a sharp, continuous outside contour line filled in with modeling which covers almost the entire surface. Conforming exactly to the surface topography, the modeling was created principally by a complex web of hachure, as in the *St. John the Baptist* drawing, or by a series of parallel wavy lines, as in the drawing after the bust *J.–P. Laurens* of 1881 (Fig. ii). This treatment had previously been confined primarily to areas of shadow as in Rodin's earliest drawing of this style in 1877 after the statue *The Age of Bronze*.[9] In the developed style of drawings after sculpture, the hachure is concentrated in deeper cavities, is less dense in smaller indentations, and thins out over projections leaving small areas of white paper which act as highlights. The densely modeled surface with small lumi-

i. *Drawing After the Statue of St. John the Baptist.* 1880. Pen and ink. 12-11/16 x 8-13/16 in. (32.2 x 22.4 cm.). Fogg Art Museum, Grenville L. Winthrop Bequest.

nous highlights suggests light reflected from a solid sculptural surface. Most sculptors' drawings of their statues are not as densely worked, although there are some exceptions such as Carpeaux's drawing of his bust *Africa*.[10] Even in Carpeaux's drawing, however, the modeling does not follow fluctuations of surface topography; this was uniquely Rodin's style adapted from modeling by profile in his sculpture. Rodin applied this original technique to drypoint portraits where the fine needle point could increase the delicacy and accuracy of the undulating hachure and the drypoint burr could add incredible richness to the complex, tactile surfaces.

Before Rodin, no sculptor had made as bold and successful a venture into printmaking. Donatello, Michelangelo, Houdon, Puget and other great sculptors in the earlier periods had not become involved in printmaking partly due to guild restrictions. The guild constraints were operative in France until the Revolution, so that the nineteenth century was the first time artists were completely free to experiment with other media. None of Rodin's three nineteenth-century predecessors, Rude, Barye or Carpeaux, were able to create an expression in the new media that was innovative or equal in power to their work in sculpture,[11] although the sculptors Maillol and Despiau, two younger contemporaries of Rodin, did distinguish themselves as printmakers.

There was much less competition in the nineteenth-century arena of sculptor-engravers than in the larger and far more active circle of painter-engravers. Rodin's technique of using long, slashed strokes in his drypoint portraits *Henri Becque* and *Victor Hugo* can be compared to the facile drypoint portrait style of Paul Helleu, a style which was continued with greater vitality by Jacques Villon. The sensuous textures of James Tissot and the subtle intricacies of Whistler also have their counterpart in Rodin's drypoint figure compositions. When Rodin's drypoints are seen in the context of nineteenth-century printmaking including Degas' monotypes, Gauguin's woodcuts, and Cezanne's etchings, they compare favorably with the work of his contemporaries who achieved, as he did, an expression in printmaking comparable in quality to their work in other media.

The combination of Rodin's repute as a sculptor and the distinctive character of his drypoints made them highly sought after for late nineteenth-century albums of original prints, although only one was ultimately included in an album. Legros wrote to ask Rodin to join him in contributing to a projected series of original print albums, saying: "I would like very much to be in your company and I

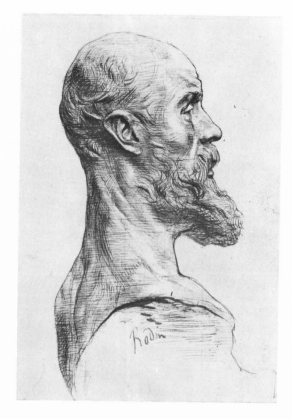

ii. *Drawing After the Bust J.–P. Laurens.* 1881. Pencil, pen and ink. 6-15/16 x 4-11/16 in. (17.6 x 11.9 cm.). British Museum.

would like you to be presented as an engraver to the English and American public. . . ."[12] Loys Delteil also wrote to Rodin about listing Rodin's name among the collaborators in the prospectus for a monthly album of original lithographs, etchings, and drypoints to be called *L'Estampe moderne*.[13] Probably occurring earlier than either of these two undated solicitations, the publication of the first album of André Marti's important volumes of *L'Estampe originale*, dated 1893,[14] included Rodin's drypoint *Henri Becque*. Rodin was one of the three artists who did not make new prints for this publication. Legros, also showing a strong desire to include Rodin's work with his in the albums, told Rodin to send a plate he had already made.

Rodin's reputation as a printmaker during the nineteenth century rests solely on the four drypoint portraits, *Victor Hugo, Three-Quarters View, Victor Hugo, Front View, Henri Becque* and *Antonin Proust*, exhibited in 1889 and 1891 at the Salon des Peintre-Graveurs[15] and published as original prints in art periodicals.[16] Since they closely resemble the bronze busts and are done in Rodin's style of drawings after sculpture, they may have been received by the general public as reproductive engravings which illustrated works of art, although connoisseurs like Roger Marx and Gustave Geffroy immediately understood their greatness. Rodin withheld the drypoint figure compositions but finally exhibited two, *La Ronde* and *Le Printemps*, along with the first drypoint portrait *Bellona*, at the Société Nationale des Beaux-Arts Salon of 1901; these three were reportedly shown only at the insistence of a friend.[17] Following this exhibition, Roger Marx made the first catalogue list of virtually all Rodin's drypoints with illustrations and some discussion for the March 1902 issue of the *Gazette des Beaux-Arts*. This article was also printed as a separate pamphlet.[18] Writing in the March 1903 issue of *The Studio*, Shaw Sparrow introduced Rodin's drypoints to the English public in an article[19] which was based on information from Alphonse Legros and possibly from Rodin himself. In December of 1902, Legros had written Rodin that he was too ill, and he could not see him when he came to London "to begin again our nice walks in the museums of London as we did twenty years ago [at the time Rodin made his first drypoint]," but that "M. Sparrow an ex-student of mine intends to publish in *The Studio* an article about your drypoint engravings. We talked a lot together about that. He is a very nice man whom I recommend to you. . . ."[20]

The first definitive catalogue of Rodin's drypoints came out as part of Loys Delteil's series on *Le Peintre-gravure illustré* of 1910.[21] Delteil depends for much of his informa-tion on Roger Marx's catalogue of 1902 and quotes extensively from Marx's article in lieu of an iconographic and stylistic discussion of his own. The Delteil volume lists all of the states of the drypoints, gives dates, measurements, illustrations of most of the states, and lists exhibitions, publications, and some collections. Delteil does not give edition sizes, information which remains difficult to ascertain, except in those situations where a drypoint was published in a limited edition book such as the *Souls of Purgatory*, printed in an edition of ninety, or where a document like the proof of *Victor Hugo, Front View* for the March 1889 *Gazette des Beaux-Arts* issue gives a notation for an edition of sixty. In general, early states of the drypoints have as few as one to five impressions while some later states, published in books or periodicals after the plate had been steel-faced, have editions from fifty to slightly over 100. A second problematic area is the chronology of Rodin's drypoints, despite the dates and information given by Roger Marx and Delteil. The problem is compounded by a letter written by Rodin to M. Bourcard in 1903[22] recalling a chronology from two previous decades which in some instances contradicts the opinions of Delteil and Roger Marx.

While it is not clear what information Delteil received from Rodin, he did meet and correspond with the artist in hopes of printing an original drypoint, *Love Turning the World*, which, however, was not included in the volume:

At the time of our last meeting you have been kind enough to promise me again to lend me the copper plate of your "Amours conduisant le monde" for my work about your engravings, as soon as you have some prints made for yourself. My work is being printed at the present and it will be published next month. . . . This printing no need to tell you I shall have made with all the necessary care and after having taken the precaution of having the plate steel-faced if it has not already been done. . . . I shall keep it only eight days and I shall bring it back to you immediately. It will be a great pleasure for me to present you with some copies of the work I have made about your engravings of which I have studied all the prints and all the states with the greatest attention. . . .[23]

This letter may also verify the information in Delteil's book that most of the copper plates, which Rodin said he possessed in 1903,[24] were still in the artist's hands in 1910. The current location of the plates is unknown; they may have been destroyed at Rodin's death.

The present catalogue raisonné of Rodin's drypoints is the first extensive iconographic and stylistic discussion of the drypoints and includes a considerable amount of comparative material, particularly related drawings found primarily among the 7,000 Rodin drawings at the Musée Rodin in Paris. The catalogue raisonné also adds the following to the work of Delteil: illustrations of more states of the drypoints; the discovery of a new first state of *Henri Becque* and a new third state of *Victor Hugo, Front View*; and two drypoints not catalogued by Delteil, *The Dying Centaur* and *Contribution Receipt of the Special American Hospital.*

1. Cladel, *Rodin,* 82.

2. Marx, *Maîtres d'Hier et d'Aujourd'hui,* chapter "Rodin Céramiste," dated 1905, 226.

3. Roger Marx explained (in "Rodin et Legros") that at Sèvres "the decoration is obtained by a process very much like intaglio; on the white sphere Rodin engraved an allegory. . . ."

4. Maillard, *Auguste Rodin, Statuaire,* 99.

5. Undated letter from Alphonse Legros to Rodin, from 57 Brook Green, Hammersmith, London W. Musée Rodin archives, Legros folder, letter no. 28. A long excerpt from this letter is given in footnote 12 below.

6. Stein, *L'Estampe originale, A Catalogue Raisonné,* 15.

7. George Bernard Shaw, "G. B. S. on Rodin," *The New York Times* (from *Nation,* London), December 1, 1912, 732.

8. George Bernard Shaw, "Rodin," *Annales politiques et littéraires,* December 2, 1932, 488.

9. *The Age of Bronze.* 1877. Pen and ink. 12 3/8 x 9-3/16 in. (31.4 x 23.3 cm.). Cabinet des Dessins, Musée du Louvre, Paris. Illustrated fig. 34 in Elsen and Varnedoe, *The Drawings of Rodin.*

10. The drawing of Carpeaux's bust *Africa* is in the collection of the Metropolitan Museum of Art, New York City. I am indebted to Dr. Kirk Varnedoe for bringing this drawing to my attention and for his list and discussion of Rodin's drawings after sculpture in Elsen and Varnedoe, *The Drawings of Rodin,* 51 and 60, figs. 34–37.

11. The prints of Rude, Barye and Carpeaux are catalogued in Delteil. One lithograph after the sculpture *Neapolitan Fisherboy* is attributed without certainty to Rude. In Barye's etching after a sculpture of a deer, his signature is scrawled awkwardly because he was unaccustomed to writing in reverse, and he emphasized fur and grass textures, capturing nothing of his tumultuous bronze surfaces which Rodin had greatly admired. Eleven lithographs by Barye parallel his fine watercolor compositions of animals in the wild but do not carry the force of his sculpture. Carpeaux offers a greater range of subject matter, etching several figure compositions, three portraits, a sketch after his sculpture *Ugolino,* etc., but his discontinuous and choppy contour lines and obvious, uninspired crosshatching do not convey his strengths as a sculptor or charm as a draftsman.

12. Undated letter from Alphonse Legros to Rodin, from 57 Brook Green, Hammersmith, London W. Musée Rodin archives, Legros folder, letter no. 28: "*Mon cher Rodin. Charles Quentin a l'intention de faire un travail sur les peintres-graveurs et je lui ai dit pourquoi pas sur les sculpteurs-graveurs aussi? Moi je vais prêter une planche pour cet ouvrage qui sera limité à un petit nombre d'artistes cinq ou six ou plus et j'aimerai beaucoup être en votre compagnie et que vous soyez présenté comme graveur au public Anglais et Américain car la graveur n'est pas autre chose que le dessin sur cuivre. Il n'y aura rien dans cette publication qui sentira le commerce c'est purement artistique; une de vos planches déjà faites fera parfaitement l'affaire. / Merci pour la présentation que vous m'avez faites de Monsieur Arsène Alexandre. . . ."*

13. Undated letter from Loys Delteil to Rodin, from 81 Blvd. du Montparnasse. Musée Rodin archives, Delteil folder: "*Paris 24 Sept. / Monsieur. Je vais faire paraître au mois de novembre prochain sous le titre l'Estampe moderne, un album mensuel de litho, eau-fortes, pointes-sèches originales. Je me permets à cette occasion de vous demander de vouloir bien m'autoriser à faire figurer votre nom parmi ceux des collaborateurs à cette publication essentiellement artistique et comme je vais faire paraître prospectus à la fin de la semaine je vous prie de vouloir bien me faire savoir votre décision aussitôt qu'il vous sera possible. Je serai très heureux lorsque vous voudrez bien faire l'appel à votre beau talent de point-séchiste. Veuillez agréer Monsieur mes sentiments très dévoués. / Loys Delteil / Artiste Graveur / 81 B. de Montparnasse.*"

14. *L'Estampe originale* was perhaps the most important print collaborative of the nineteenth century to which seventy-four well-known as well as young artists contributed ninety-five original prints in every medium of printmaking, many experimental and innovative, especially in the area of color lithography (Stein, *L'Estampe originale, A Catalogue Raisonné*). My thanks go to Donna Stein for helpful discussion on *L'Estampe originale* and nineteenth-century printmaking in general.

15. *Les Maîtres Artistes,* 284, mentions that the drypoints of Victor Hugo were exhibited under the numbers 266–269 at the Salon des Peintres-Graveurs, Galeries Durand-Ruel, January 23–February 14, 1889. Frederick Lawton (*The Life and Work of Auguste Rodin,* 100) says that all of the drypoint portraits were shown at both the 1889 and 1891 Salon des Peintres-Graveurs.

16. For the dates and periodicals in which the drypoint portraits were published see the catalogue information under each drypoint.

17. Marx, *Les Pointes Sèches de Rodin,* 8.

18. *Ibid.* See *Bibliography.*

19. Sparrow, "Auguste Rodin's Dry-Point Engravings," 88–93.

20. Letter from Legros to Rodin, dated December 31, 1902, from Woodlands, Brasted Chart, Kent. Musée Rodin archives, Legros folder, letter no. 31. "*Mon cher Rodin / Votre lettre vient de m'arriver au cottage que j'habite à la campagne et j'aurais été bien heureux de recommencer ensemble nos bonnes promenades dans les Musées de Londres comme il y a vingt ans mais je suis forcé de rester ici pour cause de santé. Quel dommage! J'aurais été enchanté de causer avec vous car je suis, comme vous savez mon cher ami, un de vos admirateurs des plus anciens et des plus dévoués. / M. Sparrow, un ancien élève à moi, a l'intention de publier dans le Studio un article sur vos gravures à la pointe sèche; nous avons beaucoup parlé de cela ensemble c'est un homme fort aimable et que je vous recommande—Je termine ce petit mot à la hâte par les compliments de la saison c'est à dire la bonne année. / Bien à vous / A. Legros.*"

21. See *Bibliography* for full reference.

22. A letter from Rodin to M. Bourcard, dated March 25, 1903, from 182, Rue de l'Université (kept in the Staatliche Museum of Berlin, Drawings and Prints Department archives) gives Rodin's chronology for the drypoints as well as some instructions for the printing or the reproduction of Rodin's drypoints: "*Cher Monsieur Bourcard / Vous trouverez ci-joint la liste que vous me demandez et que je vous envoie bien volontiers- / Recevez je vous prie mes vives cordialités. / A Rodin / N'avez vous bien gravé à la pointe sèche que les 8 pièces suivantes? Pourriez-vous me les numéroter par ordre chronologique en mettant l'année en regard S.V.P. /*

no ordre		année
2	*Victor Hugo* 3/4 *à droite*	1885
2	*Victor Hugo de face*	1885
4	*Antonin Proust*	1888
3	*Henri Becque*	1887
4	*Le Printemps*	1888
1	*La Ronde*	1884
2	*Bellone*	1885
2	*La Sphere*	1885

Les cuivres sont-ils tous détruits? Non. Je les ai encore en ma possession."

23. Letter from Delteil to Rodin, dated October 9, 1910, from 2, Rue des Beaux-Arts. Musée Rodin archives, Delteil folder. "*Cher Monsieur, / Lors de notre dernière entrevue, vous avez bien voulu me promettre à nouveau le prêt de votre cuivre des 'Les Amours conduisant le monde' pour mon livre sur votre œuvre gravé, aussitôt que vous auriez fait tirer pour vous-même quelques épreuves. Mon travail est en ce moment à l'impression et il paraîtra le mois prochain . . . tirage que je ferai faire je n'ai pas besoin de vous le dire à nouveau avec tous les soins possibles et après avoir pris la précaution de faire acierer la planche si ce n'est déjà fait. . . . Je ne la garderai que 8 jours et vous la rapporterai aussitôt. Je me ferai un grand plaisir de vous offrir des exemplaires du travail que j'ai établi sur votre œuvre gravé dont j'ai étudié avec le plus grand soin toutes les pièces et tous les états. / Je vous prie d'agréer cher Monsieur l'expression de mes sentiments respectueux. / Loys Delteil.*"

24. In the last paragraph of the letter (given in footnote 22 above) Rodin says that he still possesses the copper plates for the drypoints.

I. Les Amours Conduisant le Monde (Love Turning the World). 1881.

8 x 9⅞ in. (20.3 x 25 cm.)

State One
1 Victoria and Albert Museum.
Mark of the plate maker at upper right.

State Two
2 Victoria and Albert Museum.
Plate mark erased.
Colls: Bibliothèque Nationale (two impressions: one on Japan paper, one on laid paper); Boston Museum of Fine Arts (heavy Japan paper); British Museum; Cleveland Museum of Art (wove vellum paper); Metropolitan Museum of Art (heavy Japan paper); Musée Rodin; National Gallery of Art, Washington; National Museum of Western Art, Tokyo; Staatliche Kunstsammlungen, Dresden; Städelsches Kunstinstitut, Frankfurt; Stadtköln, Wallraf-Richartz Museum; Szépmüvészeti Múzeum, Budapest; University of Glasgow Museum (laid paper).

It is often said that Rodin made his first drypoint, *Love Turning the World*, with an ordinary sewing needle[1] on the back of a plate by Alphonse Legros while visiting him in England in 1881.[2] The back of the plate still bore the mark of the plate maker. Rodin left it on the plate for the first state (Fig. 1) but scraped the plate mark off for the second (Fig. 2), virtually the only difference between the two states. Rodin's designation of this drypoint as "*La sphere— 1885*" in his letter of 1903 to M. Bourcard may refer to the second state.

Starting with a frieze of nine putti, he added a globe and clouds to create the illusion that some of the putti were coming out of the clouds while the other romping putti turn the world. Their turning motion is more convincing than the globe's because the sculptor suggests movement more successfully through his figures than through the setting. The figures, placed approximately on the same plane, each appear to take a variant of the position of jumping with their arms raised to a near shoulder level so that, as the viewer looks from one to the next, the illusion of a succession of movement is created.[3] It was natural for the sculptor to draw the figures of the putti in different views since this was his method in sculpture of modeling successive profiles of the figure as he rotated the clay stand.

As a source for the drypoint, Rodin may have recalled

modeling or walking around one of his several putti statues like *L'Idylle d'Ixelles* of 1876[4] which he had done for architectural and small scale decorations during the 1870's. The third putto from the right in *Love Turning the World* relates to both the standing child of *L'Idylle d'Ixelles* and the putto in the drawing *Standing Putto* (MR 93). Also, a number of drawings from the 1860's or 1870's of putti alone or in groups could have served Rodin as a store of images.[5]

The composition of a circle of amours among the clouds might have come from a common seventeenth- and eighteenth-century motif such as Fragonard's *Circle of Amours*.[6] Or, Rodin may have seen allegorical compositions with amours and a globe like Carpeaux's etching *Geometry of Decartes*.[7] Rodin worked with similar allegories in his traditional decorative work at Sèvres, most of which includes amours dancing or looking out from clouds or a landscape.[8] The title of the drypoint and the idea of amours turning the world (or love making the world go round) was probably Rodin's own, for in 1908 he had written an almost identical title, "*Les enfants amours conduisant le monde. . .*"[9] on one impression of the print, and the title had also been listed by Roger Marx in his 1902 catalogue of Rodin's drypoints.

Two drawings are related to the drypoint's composition, a sketch of eight amours on top of a globe held up by a nude woman (Fig. 3) and *Two Putti Turning the World* (Fig. 4) in which two cherubs hold up a globe that appears to rotate.[10] The style of the second drawing is also very similar to that of the drypoint. In both the drawing and the drypoint, contour lines block out the chubby bodies, one line dividing the back and others squaring off the buttocks; heavy black dots mark the facial features and dimples; and loose, sketchy lines, roughly parallel but not carefully aligned, cover areas to create an atmospheric tonality while others curve to model volumes. The parallel lines show the combined influence of Legros' engraving technique and the characteristic mode of Rodin's drawings of the period.

I

2

19

3

4

1. The expediency of using a sewing needle was in character with Rodin's occasional use at Sèvres of a cut-off pocket knife attached to a stick to incise relief. His use of a pocket knife was witnessed by a fellow worker and recorded by Roger Marx in *Maîtres d'Hier et d'Aujourd'hui*, 226.

2. Sparrow, "Auguste Rodin's Dry-Point Engravings," 92. Like most sources, Sparrow gives the date of 1881 for Rodin's trip to England. The work records from the Sèvres Porcelain Manufactory show three breaks when Rodin might have been in England: June–August 1881, November 1881, and January–September 1882 (Marx, *Auguste Rodin, Céramiste*, 43).

3. During his career Rodin had developed various solutions in sculpture and drawing to a contemporary problem of depicting motion in art. This problem is discussed in Thorson, *The Late Drawings of Auguste Rodin*, 50–101.

4. Grappe, no. 34.

5. See RELATED DRAWINGS.

6. Albert Elsen has said that this drypoint "may have been based specifically upon Fragonard's *Ronde d'Amours*, or its interpretation in an aquatint by Jean-Claude Richard de Saint Non"; the Saint Non print is reproduced in F. Courboin, *La Gravure en France des origines à 1900*, Paris: Librairie Delagrave, 1923, 122 (Elsen, "Rodin's 'La Ronde'," 294).

7. Delteil, no. 7, *Projet d'Encadrement pour la géometrie de Decartes*, 1860.

8. Marx, *Auguste Rodin, Céramiste;* see especially vase *l'Hiver*, pls. III and IV.

9. The full inscription of the print, in the collection of the National Gallery of Art, Washington, is "*Les enfants amours conduisant le monde / A Madame Simpson affectueusement / Aug. Rodin / 1908*."

10. According to Dr. Kirk Varnedoe, Fig. 4 is based on a sketch of two men supporting a globe (MR 167. Pencil. 4 x 2-13/16 in., [10.2 x 7.1 cm.]), which in turn has its source in a work Rodin sketched while in Italy, for it was drawn on a sheet from a notebook probably taken to Italy in 1875.

RELATED DRAWINGS

3   *Woman Supporting Globe Encircled by Amours*. 1880–1881. Pencil, pen and brown ink, brown wash. 6-13/16 x 3-3/16 in. (17.3 x 8.1 cm.). Stanford University Museum of Art, gift of Mme. Lascelle de Basily. Inscribed "*A Madame de Basily Collemaki, affectueusement, Rodin*."

4   *Two Putti Turning the World*. c. 1875–1881. Pen and ink, gray wash, spots of white gouache. 3-15/16 x 2¾ in. (10 x 7 cm.). MR 141.

RELATED DRAWINGS NOT REPRODUCED
Standing Putto. c. 1854–1864. Pencil, black ink background. 4-1/16 x 2⅝ in. (10.3 x 6.7 cm.). MR 93.

Putto Facing Left. 1854–1864. Pencil. 4¼ x 1¾ in. (10.8 x 4.4 cm.). MR 116. Other early drawings (c. 1854–1864) of putti are MR 21, 22, 23, 29, 36, 41, 92.

REPRODUCTIONS (in Rodin's lifetime)
Cladel, *Auguste Rodin, lœuvre et l'homme*, opp. 142.
Delteil, no. 1.
Les Maîtres Artistes, between 292 and 293.
The Studio, March 1903, 89.

II. Etudes des Figures (Figure Studies). 1881.

8⅞ x 6⅞ in. (22.5 x 17.5 cm.)

Unique State

5   Victoria and Albert Museum.
Coll: Kunsthalle, Bremen.
An impression of the plate canceled by the artist (1885.
8-11/16 x 5⅞ in. [22 x 15 cm.]) is in the private collection
of Mr. and Mrs. Laurence Brunswick, Jr., Rydal, Pennsylvania, and another is in the British Museum.

Roger Marx lists *Figure Studies* (Fig. 5) as Rodin's second
drypoint, dating it 1881, the same year as *Love Turning the
World*. Rodin used the subject of playing children in both
prints, and the style of the drypoints shows the same
uneven pressure in handling the graving needle which is
particularly noticeable in the spotty contour lines of the
nude woman in the center of *Figure Studies*.

Very few impressions of this print were pulled, and the
plate was canceled by 1884 when the other side was used
for *Victor Hugo, Three-Quarters View*. The print was never
shown or reproduced until it appeared in Delteil's catalogue
in 1910. These facts confirm the experimental nature of
the plate, supported also by the evidence that the six figures are not related in one composition. The four figures
in the upper portion of the print appear to have been the
nucleus for a typical Sèvres design. A gracefully elongated
female nude seen from the back contrasts with her muscular male counterpart seen in profile; their hands stretch out
to join in a bacchic revel or an embrace, while two jostling
nude babies look on.[1] Having given up on a unified composition, Rodin drew two fantastic or allegorical heads on
the lower half of the plate.

Without interrupting the lines of the woman's legs,
Rodin created the right head starting from the ground line
under her feet which became an awkward backbone or
hairline. Both heads are reminiscent of the "black" gouache drawings: they freely combine nightmarish fantasies
from literary sources, such as Dante's *Inferno*, with sug-
gestions of classical allegories of war. The right head shows
a small reclining figure on her war helmet while the left
has a snake around her neck, not unlike Minerva who
wears on her chest plate a Medusa head with snakes for
hair. Rodin also used the Medusa head in a drawing during this period[2] and later in 1896 in a marble head executed

by his workshop called *Minerva* which bore the Medusa
head.[3]

The right head is probably based on Rodin's sketch of a
frontal view of a bust with a small reclining figure on her
helmet (Fig. 6). A second drawing of a helmeted head in
profile (Fig. 7) is heavily layered with black wash and
spotted with white gouache giving it a frightening Dantesque countenance which appears in the heads of the drypoint as hollow black eye sockets and crude, bold modeling, particularly in the left head.

1. Marx, *Auguste Rodin, Céramiste*, vase *l'Aire et l'Eau*, pl. II.
2. *Les Dessins d'Auguste Rodin*.
3. Grappe, no. 283.

5

6   7

RELATED DRAWINGS
6   *Allegorical Head with Figure on Helmet.* c. 1870–1881.
Charcoal, pen and purple-blue ink on graph paper. 7⅝ x
4⅝ in. (19.4 x 11.7 cm.). MR 380.

7   *Profile Head with Helmet.* c. 1875–1881. Pen and ink,
black wash, white gouache. 4-15/16 x 2⅜ in. (12.5 x 6 cm.).
MR 5619.

REPRODUCTIONS (in Rodin's lifetime)
Delteil, no. 2.

III. Buste de Bellone
(Bust of Bellona). 1882-1885.
5-13/16 x 3-15/16 in. (14.8 x 10 cm.)

State One
8   Klingler Collection.
Before fullness added to hair at left; hair hangs straight
down and flat against side of head.
Coll: Musée Rodin.

State Two
9   Musée Rodin.
Additions to hair at left but dark silhouette of original
shape of hair in state 1 is still clear; additions to hair at
right; new modeling in face and neck darkening shadows;
cluster of small circles added to helmet ornaments at right.

State Three
10   Victoria and Albert Museum.
Signed "A Rodin."
Additions to hair at left so that dark silhouette of original
shape of hair in state 1 is blended with added strands of
hair; edges of plate still rough.
Colls: Metropolitan Museum of Art (acc. no. 16.37.3, laid
paper); Musée Rodin (inscribed "*à ma femme Aug Rodin*");
Pasadena Art Museum; Stadtköln, Wallraf-Richartz
Museum (heavy Japan paper).

11   National Gallery of Art, Washington, gift of Mrs.
John W. Simpson.
Inscribed "*Portrait de Mme Rodin / à Madame J. W. Kate
Simpson affectueusement / Aug Rodin 1908.*"
Plate beveled to eliminate rough edges.
Colls: The Fine Arts Museums of San Francisco (China
paper, signed "A Rodin"); Fogg Art Museum (white wove
paper); Metropolitan Museum of Art (two impressions:
acc. no. 29.52.8, signed "A Rodin" and 64.560, vellum
paper); Minneapolis Institute of Arts (signed "A Rodin");
National Museum of Western Art, Tokyo; Princeton Uni-
versity Art Museum; St. Louis Art Museum; Toledo
Museum of Art.

Copied from Rodin's bronze bust *Bellona* (Fig. 12), god-
dess of war, the head of Bellona in the drypoint (Fig. 8) is
a more conventional allegory than the grotesque and freely
drawn allegorical heads in the drypoint *Figure Studies*. The
bust was submitted in 1879 to a competition for a sculp-

8

9

10

11

12

ture symbolizing the French Republic and was not accepted. Grappe dates the terra-cotta bust 1878 since the
sculpture competition was held in the beginning of the
year 1879; he dates a bronze version 1881,[1] the same date
given by Judith Cladel.[2] The drypoint, then, could con-
ceivably date from 1881. Delteil's criterion for dating it 1883
is that he gives 1883 as the date for the bronze. Roger
Marx lists the drypoint *Bellona* as Rodin's third, recognizing the artist's greater confidence in handling the drypoint
needle than in his first two prints but pointing out the
lingering influence of Legros in the regularity of the parallel and diagonal hachure (see Frontispiece). In his letter to
M. Bourcard of 1903, Rodin dates the drypoint *Bellona*
1885.

The model for the sculpture bust of Bellona was Rose
Beuret, who was thirty-four in 1878 when the bust was
made. She lived with Rodin as his mistress from 1864, bore
him a son in 1866, and finally married him in 1917 shortly
before they both died.

That the drypoint *Bellona* was copied from the *Bust of
Bellona's* frontal view is clearly seen from the first state of the
drypoint where the hair is flattened on one side of the head
and appears reversed in position from the bust; other details
are also reversed, such as the higher shoulder which bears a
fragment of armor or drapery. The drypoint follows the
frontal view of the bust where the flaring nostrils and tight
set of the chin, which give the bust its fierce, warlike expression, are less prominent than in the bust's side view.
Rodin softened the stormy, brooding allegory of war to
achieve a more intimate portrait of his wife in the drypoint.
The artist wrote the title "*Portrait de Mme. Rodin*" on one
print of *Bellona* as part of a dedication inscription written in
1908 (Fig. 11) and on another print kept in his own collection and now in the Musée Rodin he wrote "*à ma femme
Aug Rodin.*"

The somber feeling was intensified by copying the bronze
with the light source coming from above so that the helmet
completely casts the eyes in shadow and darkens the creases
around the mouth. The shadows on the face and neck contrast with the large illuminated area below, leaving the
shoulders and breasts less carefully defined and more awkward than in the bust. Rodin appears to exaggerate the lights
and darks in this early drypoint to create a strong sense of
sculptural mass, an effect he achieved in the later drypoints
with greater subtlety.

In the first state of *Bellona*, Rodin copied the severe line of
the sculpture's hair which is flattened against the sides of the
face, while in the second and third states (Figs. 9 and 10)
changes were made primarily to augment the fullness of the

hair, the shadows on the face, and to increase the softness
and flow of motion in the image. The greater freedom in the
twisted, flowing locks which were added contrasts with the
unchanged area of tighter parallel lines below and points to
a new stylistic direction in the drypoint portraits that follow.

1. Grappe, nos. 44 and 45.
2. Cladel, *Auguste Rodin, l'œuvre et l'homme*, 157.

RELATED SCULPTURE
12   *Bust of Bellona*. 1881. Bronze. H. 32 in. (81.3 cm.). Stanford University Museum of Art, gift of the B. G. Cantor
Art Foundation.

REPRODUCTIONS (in Rodin's lifetime)
Bénédite, "Propos sur Rodin," 32 (state 2 reproduced);
same article in *L'Art et les Artistes*, 90.
Cladel, *Auguste Rodin*, opp. 152.
Delteil, no. 3.
Les Maîtres Artistes, between 292 and 293.

IV. Le Printemps
(Allegory of Spring). 1882-1888.
5-13/16 x 3-15/16 in. (14.8 x 10 cm.)

Unique State
13   Victoria and Albert Museum.
Printed in dark brown, red-brown and black ink; printed
in black ink and included as an original print for Marx,
"Les Pointes Sèches de Rodin," opp. 204, and in black ink
on laid paper for the separate pamphlet, Marx, *Les Pointes
Sèches de Rodin,* opp. 12.
Colls: Art Institute of Chicago (laid paper); Bibliothèque
Nationale (two impressions: one dark brown ink on laid
paper, one black ink on Japan paper); Boston Museum of
Fine Arts (heavy Japan paper); British Museum; Cantor,
Fitzgerald Art Foundation; Cleveland Museum of Art;
Metropolitan Museum of Art (signed "A Rodin"); Min-
neapolis Institute of Arts (two impressions: acc. no. 6932;
acc. no. 12, 798 on Japan paper); Museum of Modern Art;
Musée Rodin (vellum paper, excellent impression);
National Museum of Western Art, Tokyo; Princeton Uni-
versity Art Museum; Rhode Island School of Design
Museum of Art; St. Louis Art Museum; Staatliche Kunst-
sammlungen, Dresden; Stadtköln, Wallraf-Richartz
Museum; Philadelphia Museum of Art (impression still in
Marx, *Les Pointes Sèches de Rodin*).

The drypoint *Le Printemps* (Fig. 13) is the reverse image of
La Nuit, a motif from Rodin's *Pompei* vase made at Sèvres.
The motif, a nude woman encircled by amours, was also
applied to a ceramic plaque (Fig. 14).[1] Records at the
Sèvres Porcelain Manufactory show Rodin working on
the vase on and off from December 1880, indicating that
the drypoint could date from 1882.[2] However, the vase had
been given to Rodin when it had become defective in fir-
ing, so that the artist could have copied it, or made the
drypoint from a lost drawing of the vase, some time after
1882. In his letter to M. Bourcard written in 1903, Rodin
dates the drypoint as late as 1888.

An earlier interpretation of Spring as a draped mother
playfully lifting a baby is represented in a drawing inscribed
"*Le Printemps,*" dated 1878.[3] The subject appears to have
evolved in the Sèvres vases *Femme et Enfant* and *Faune et
Enfant*[4] as a nude woman with a child on her shoulder, and
in the *Pompei* vase as a nude woman with a circle of winged
babies around her head. Roger Marx interprets the motif
on the *Pompei* vase as the dual iconography of Venus and

Spring: "Venus crowned with Amours who whisper their
secrets in the drunkenness of a spring morning."[5] Without
the vase's more elaborate symbolism, the nude figure with
putti when isolated on the plaque and drypoint appears
as a simple Toilet of Venus with cupids attending. However, the sentiment of the woman's maternal embrace of
the baby along with the title *Le Printemps,* given the drypoint in 1901 when it was first shown, suggests the same
dual meaning of Venus and Spring present in the vase.

Rodin worked out the positions of Venus and the putti
in the preparatory drawings for the vase (Figs. 15 and 16).
In the earlier composition (Fig. 16) Venus is turned side-
ways and surrounded by an aureole-shaped chain of
amours climbing and flying up to her shoulders from the
ground. By the time the composition is developed for the
drypoint, all of the putti cluster around her head, and her
body becomes the central spoke around which a dynamic
ring of putti revolves. Background slashes, both curved
and in rows of horizontal and diagonal strokes, are still
reminiscent of Legros but are now more freely drawn. The
dynamism and movement of these counterbalancing
strokes in combination with the salient light projections
and rich, soft textured blacks, which allow the forms to
dissolve into darkness, attest to an eloquence and a technical mastery and may corroborate Rodin's late date of 1888
for the drypoint.

Possibly in response to the excitement of multiplying his
images through printmaking, Rodin took the image of
Le Printemps and experimented with a common reproductive method, the ancestor of today's mimeograph and of
the French "Reniotype" machine, commonly used for
printing menus. Drawing several versions of *Le Printemps,*
Rodin reproduced some by machine, reinforcing with a pen
those lines which had grown faint in reproduction (Fig. 17).
The machine process was the same one used for form letters
dating to 1887[6] sent to Rodin from organizations such as the
Union Centrale des Arts Décoratifs. These were also done
in purple-blue ink printed on thin inexpensive paper and
were overwirtten by hand where the words were faint. At
the Musée Rodin there are about six different versions of *Le
Printemps* produced in this way and about ten sheets of two
other subjects using the same technique. Rodin's machine
reproductions of a few of his drawings, though unique and
interesting as newly discovered "prints," are much less
valuable as works of art.

1. Marx, *Auguste Rodin, Céramiste,* plaque *La Nuit,* pl. XV.
2. *Ibid.,* 43.
3. Elsen and Varnedoe, *The Drawings of Rodin,* reproduced fig. 33.

428

13

4. Marx, *Auguste Rodin, Céramiste*, vase *Femme et Enfant*, pl. VI; and vase *Faune et Enfant*, pl. VII.

5. Marx, *Maîtres d'Hier et d'Aujourd'hui*, 232.

6. Form letter from Antonin Proust to Rodin, dated May 17, 1887. Musée Rodin archives, Proust folder.

RELATED DRAWINGS

14 *La Nuit*. 1880–1882. Porcelain plaque. 4 1/8 x 3 1/8 in. (10.5 x 8 cm.). Designed by Rodin at Sèvres Porcelain Manufactory. Inscribed "*à Sèvres 1880 / Auguste Rodin / Décembre 1907 / à mon amie la Comtesse Basily Callimaki*." Stanford University Museum of Art, gift of Mme. Lascelle de Basily. (Photograph by Becky Cohen).

15 *Le Printemps*. 1880. Pen and ink. Location and dimensions unknown. Reproduced from *La Plume*, special issue devoted to Rodin, 1900, 57.

16 *Woman with Aureole of Eight Putti*. 1800. Pen and ink, gray wash. 6-1/16 x 3-15/16 in. (15.4 x 10 cm.). MR 6329.

17 *Profile Nude Woman Holding Child*. 1882–1883. Purple-blue ink, reproductive technique with pen and ink lines over. 5 3/8 x 8-1/16 in. (13.7 x 20.5 cm.). MR 5929.

RELATED DRAWINGS NOT REPRODUCED

Front View Nude Woman with Four Putti. 1882–1883. Purple-blue ink, reproductive technique. MR 435.

Woman with Four Putti. 1882–1883. Purple-blue ink, reproductive technique. 6-13/16 x 3-9/16 in. (17.3 x 9 cm.). MR 436.

Nude Woman with Putti. 1882–1883. Purple-blue ink, reproductive technique. 5 1/4 x 3-3/16 in. (13.3 x 8 cm.). MR 441.

Nude Woman with Amours. 1882–1883. Purple-blue ink, reproductive technique. 5 1/4 x 4 in. (13.3 x 10.2 cm.). MR 452.

Nude Woman in Profile with Winged Putti. 1882–1883. Purple-blue ink, reproductive technique. 8 1/4 x 4 1/4 in. (21 x 10.8 cm.). MR 454.

REPRODUCTIONS (in Rodin's lifetime)

L'Art et les Artistes, 28.

Delteil, no. 4.

Sparrow, "Auguste Rodin's Dry-Point Engravings," 88.

14

15

16

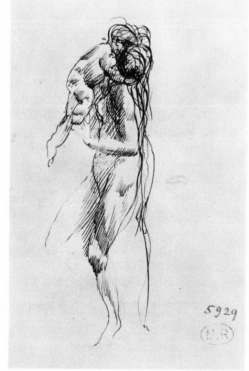

17

V. La Ronde
(The Round). 1883-1884.
9 x 7 in. (22.9 x 17.8 cm.)

State One

18   The Fine Arts Museums of San Francisco (Japan paper).
Scratches on plate visible; all of plate inked or with narrow
margins, so scratches visible, especially in large area below
image (Delteil, state 2).
Colls: British Museum; Musée Rodin (signed "A Rodin");
National Gallery of Art, Washington (inscribed "*à mon viel
ami Gustave Geffroy / A Rodin*"); Staatliche Kunstsammlungen, Dresden.

19   Staatliche Graphische Sammlung, Munich.
Scratches not visible; margins and large area below image
wiped clean of ink; corners of plate still sharp (Delteil,
state 1).
Colls: Bibliothèque Nationale; Cleveland Museum of Art;
Minneapolis Institute of Arts (printed in green ink, signed
"A Rodin").

State Two

20   Museum of Fine Arts, Boston, gift of Mr. and Mrs.
Peter A. Wick.
Sharp corners of plate rounded; burr worn.
Colls: Art Institute of Chicago (laid paper, signed "A
Rodin"); Musée Rodin (laid paper); Stadtköln, Wallraf-
Richartz Museum; Staatliche Graphische Sammlung,
Munich.

State Three

21   Bibliothèque Nationale.
Plate beveled; letters AA lower right corner; printed in
black ink and included as an original print in *L'Art et les
Artistes*, 2 (table of contents of the issue lists "*La Ronde, pointe
sèche originale, inédite, de A. Rodin*"). Delteil calls the impression a heliogravure.
Coll: Cantor, Fitzgerald Art Foundation.

The drypoint *La Ronde* (Fig. 18) depicts seven nude muscular men holding hands in a circle dance, observed by small
groups of figures on either side, set in an open plane with
mountains and a church spire sparsely indicated in the distance. Roger Marx lists the drypoint as Rodin's fifth, following the prints of 1881–1882, as it was done at a time
when Rodin was able to translate into drypoint his personal
and expressive "black" drawing style with a controlled
mastery of the drypoint needle. According to Marx, "the
drypoint has become the docile instrument of his impulsive
drawing and his vast inspiration."[1] Delteil dates *La Ronde*
"1883?", and Rodin gives the date of 1884 in his letter to
M. Bourcard.

The prototype drawing for *La Ronde*, now preserved in
the collection of Claude Roger-Marx, was examined last
year by Dr. Kirk Varnedoe who, in describing it, says, "To
the best of my recollection, the drawing shows the groups
in the same size and substantially in the same composition as
the print. The drawing is in pen and ink on tracing paper.
The most substantial difference lies in the background. In
the drawing, the dancing circle seems more in depth, less
frieze-like than in the print, and the deep space is filled with
a series of high arch structures, suggesting a courtyard or
perhaps the interior of a cathedral."[2]

This latest discovery supports one of Prof. Albert Elsen's
interpretations in his comprehensive article "Rodin's 'La
Ronde.' " If the setting in the final sketch for *La Ronde* were
a cathedral, an idea carried into the print by the small church
spire, Rodin may have considered his imagery to be the
irreverent round dance of the witches' Sabbath which took
place inside a cathedral in nineteenth-century examples of
the subject.[3] In three "black" drawings of the 1880's
inscribed "*sabbat*" and "*aube retour du sabbat*" ("return from
the Sabbath at dawn") Rodin showed the sexual ride of
witches to and from the Sabbath by three women mounted
on a broom, a centaur, and a hybrid snake.[4] This clear evidence of Rodin's familiarity with the witches' Sabbath
imagery makes plausible the possibility that *La Ronde* represents the climactic event when, after the feast, there is a round
dance which ends in a sexual orgy.

Of Rodin's many drawings of figures in a round dance or
clasping hands and moving in a line (from his early period
and 1870–1885), none were actually inscribed "*sabbat*," and
only the presence of a possible cathedral interior in the definitive drawing for *La Ronde* in the Claude Roger-Marx
collection and the exterior church spire in the final drypoint
provide specific links with the event.

There are two drawings which can be added to those

18

19

already known to relate to *La Ronde*. One depicts four male nudes in a round dance with a woman behind the group playing with a child (Fig. 22). Her presence gives the composition a lyrical mood which is also the tone of the other drawing (Fig. 23), a composition close to the Sèvres vase *Danse de Sylvains*[5] where the meaning is clearly a bacchic revel. Another source for *La Ronde* given by Prof. Elsen is Dante's *Inferno*, a text which inspired numerous "black" drawings, some inscribed "Dante" or "*Dante et Virgile. . . .*" According to Prof. Elsen, *La Ronde* may embody Dante's imagery of the torment of homosexuals who must move eternally under rains of fiery sand and who were observed by Dante and Virgil to be turning in a circle. Dr. Elsen also suggests that *La Ronde* may represent Rodin's "desire to create a modern Dance of Death . . ." in view of the following evidence: (1) a drawing of a round dance of male nudes encircling a tomb; (2) the idea that the seated spectators of *La Ronde* may carry the same tragic connotation as the seated naked male figures in his drawings and sculptures such as *The Thinker*; and (3) a "literal meaning of la ronde . . . [as] each in his turn, which can allude to everyman's death."[6]

A dance of death was shown in the drawing *Death and the Maiden* (Fig. 102a) as an illustration for Baudelaire's *Les Fleurs du Mal*. In another drawing of the same theme, Death viperously attacks the prostrated body of a woman (Fig. 88b). Both drawings attest to Rodin's profound apprehension of the inevitable toll of death, which is probably the thematic connotation of *La Ronde's* heavy, joyless dance of male nudes.

1. Marx, *Les Pointes Sèches de Rodin*, 8.
2. Dr. Kirk Varnedoe, New York City, note written September 1974.
3. *La Ronde du Sabbat*, by Louis Boulanger, fig. 16 in Albert Elsen, "Rodin's 'La Ronde.'"
4. For illustrations and discussion of these drawings see Thorson, "Symbolism and Conservatism in Rodin's Late Drawings," in Elsen and Varnedoe, *The Drawings of Rodin*, 127–135.
5. Elsen, "Rodin's 'La Ronde,'" fig. 9.
6. *Ibid.*, 297–298

22

23

36

22 *Male Nude Dancers with a Woman and Child.* 1879–1884. Pencil pen and ink, gray wash. 3 ⅛ x 3-9/16 in. (8 x 9 cm.). MR 1937.

23 *Circle Dance of Six Male Nudes.* c. 1870–1880. Pencil, gray ink wash, graph paper, mounted on a printed page. 4⅝ x 7⅛ in. (11.7 x 18 cm.). MR 1951.

Four Nude Men in Round Dance. c. 1870. Pencil, 3¾ x 3⅝ in. (9.5 x 9.2 cm.). MR 427.

Four Male Nudes with Clasped Hands Moving in a Line. c. 1870–1875. Pencil, pen and ink. 3⅝ x 3¾ in. (9.2 x 9.5 cm.). MR 1940.

Seven Male Nudes Dancing in a Circle. c. 1875–1884. Pencil. 3 x 3½ in. (7.6 x 8.9 cm.). Collection of Mrs. Jane Wade Lombard, New York. Reproduced in Elsen, "Rodin's 'La Ronde,'" fig. 10.

Study for a Tomb Project with Male Nudes Encircling Tomb. c. 1875–1884. Pencil, ink wash. 2-15/16 x 3-5/16 in. (7.5 x 8.4 cm.). MR 5622. Reproduced in Elsen, "Rodin's 'La Ronde,'" fig. 11, and in *Les Dessins d'Auguste Rodin.*

Three Male Nudes in Circle Dance with One Seated Male Nude at the Right. c. 1875–1884. Pencil, gray wash (on mount with other drawings). 1⅜ x 1-15/16 in. (3.5 x 4.9 cm.). MR 5608. Reproduced in Elsen, "Rodin's 'La Ronde,'" fig. 12, and in *Les Dessins d'Auguste Rodin.*

Three Male Nudes and a Fiddler. c. 1875–1884. Pencil, ink wash. 3-13/16 x 5¼ in. (9.7 x 13.3 cm.). MR 5621. Reproduced in Elsen, "Rodin's 'La Ronde,'" fig. 13. Dr. Kirk Varnedoe thinks that this composition may have been taken from the bas relief of the *Tomb of Marie Antonie delle Torre,* by Andrea Riccio, in the Louvre, invoice no. OAO99, since Rodin had copied other figures from this group of reliefs. Dr. Varnedoe feels that "the memory of this group figured among the prototypes for Rodin's *La Ronde*" (from a discussion, September 1974, New York City).

Two Women and One Man in Circle Dance with Putto on Altar. c. 1864–1870. Pen and ink. 2⅞ x 4½ in. (7.3 x 11.4 cm.). MR 75.

Five Women in a Row Dancing. c. 1874–1880. Charcoal. 4½ x 7⅝ in. (11.4 x 19.4 cm.). MR 1939. Dr. Varnedoe called my attention to the fact that this composition was redrawn probably in 1907 for Roger Marx in connection with his book *Auguste Rodin, Céramiste.* The version of the drawing for Roger Marx is now in a private collection in Palo Alto.

Four Women in a Circle Dance. c. 1864–1874. Pencil, charcoal and white gouache. 4⅝ x 7¼ in. (11.7 x 18.4 cm.). MR 1944.

REPRODUCTIONS (in Rodin's lifetime)
Cladel, *Auguste Rodin,* opp. 144.
Delteil, no. 5.
Les Maîtres Artistes, between 292 and 293.
Marx, *Les Pointes Sèches de Rodin,* 15; same article in *Gazette de Beaux-Arts,* 204.

VI. L'Amphore
(Amphora). 1883-1885.
8¾ x 6-3/16 in. (22.2 x 15.9 cm.)

Unique State
24   British Museum.
Coll: Musée Rodin.
An impression with plate canceled by the artist is in the
Musée Rodin.

The large amphora and smaller marginal sketches were
engraved on the back of a plate marred with scratches and
pit marks (Fig. 24). The plate was canceled when the clearer
reverse surface was used for *Victor Hugo, Front View*, dated
1885. The series of three horsemen at the top of the
plate is often compared with Rodin's plaster model for the
equestrian monument to General Lynch, usually dated
1886,[1] although the series also resembles sketches of horsemen in the archives of the Musée Rodin. The diverse studies
give the print the appearance of a notebook page which
could have been made earlier or worked on over a period of
time, since Rodin was in the habit of returning to drawings made years earlier. In the right-hand margin, the lines
of two of the horsemen are drawn over the faint sketches
of two male busts, a figure recalled from one of Michelangelo's slaves and a tiny mounted putto or bacchus. The tiny
figure rides a lion or griffin, also the subject of several
sketches in the Musée Rodin, and is the cover ornament for
a faintly drawn urn with square handles which was later
transformed into the large round amphora.

The amphora shape, as well as a small faint vase with one
handle at the right margin, are typical of vase shapes used
by Carriére-Belleuse, for whom Rodin worked as a deco-
rator on and off from 1864 to 1882, which included Rodin's
period at the Sèvres Manufactory. The abstract leaf
design at the top and the bottom of the vase and a ring of
circling figures appealed to Rodin as early as his student
years when he copied a vase from Pergamon at the Louvre.[2]
The circling band of muscular male nudes is typical of both
the Sèvres bacchic dances[3] and his numerous sketches of
this motif from the 1870's and 1880's, a motif which was
developed as the principal subject of his drypoint *La Ronde*.

1. Grappe, no. 163.
2. K. Varnedoe, "Early Drawings by Auguste Rodin," *Burlington Magazine*, April 1974, 197, fig. 37.
3. Roger Marx, *Auguste Rodin, Céramiste*, vase *Farandole bacchique*, pl.
VIII; and vase *Pompei*, pl. XII.

RELATED DRAWINGS NOT REPRODUCED
Rider on Rearing Horse. c. 1864. Pen and ink, gray wash.
4¼ x 5 in. (10.8 x 12.7 cm.). MR 460.
Rider on Galloping Horse. c. 1864–1870. Pencil, pen and ink,
watercolor wash. 4-3/16 x 4½ in. (10.6 x 11.4 cm.). MR 152.
Putto Riding Griffin. c. 1864–1874. Pencil, pen and ink.
3-13/16 x 3-13/16 in. (9.7 x 9.7 cm.). MR 367.
Man Riding a Lion. c. 1864–1874. Pencil, black lines applied
with brush. 4 x 5 ⅞ in. (10.2 x 14.9 cm.). MR 371.
Putto Riding a Lion. c. 1864–1874. Pen and ink. 3¼ x
3-15/16 in. (8.3 x 10 cm.). MR 442.

REPRODUCTIONS (in Rodin's lifetime)
Delteil, no. 8.

24

VII. Henri Becque. 1883-1887.
6¼ x 8 in. (15.9 x 20.3 cm.)

State One
25   The Cleveland Museum of Art, gift of the Folio Club in honor of Henry S. Francis (laid paper).
Silhouette of the sculpture bust and details such as the bow ties still clearly visible (not catalogued by Delteil).

State Two
26   National Gallery of Art, Washington.
Inscribed *"Becque/ à Monsieur Cardon/ amitié Rodin."*
Series of diagonal lines added to shoulder of left figure; long lines added across neck and chest of center figure; new work behind heads (Delteil, state 1).
Coll: British Museum.

State Three
27   Collection unknown. Reproduced from Delteil.
Inscribed *"à mon ami Bracquemond."*
Left figure has new modeling on forehead and several long lines from neck across shoulder; right figure, lines added to ear and one vertical and one diagonal line to shoulder; diagonal line upper left background (Delteil, state 2).

State Four
28   R. M. Light & Company, Inc., Boston.
Signed "Aug Rodin."
Left head moustache filled out; vertical line added to back of head and more lines drawn on shoulder; right figure ten long curving lines added to shoulder; above impression one of several before plate worn; worn plate was printed in black ink with half-inch margins on laid paper with "Arches" watermark and included as an original print in the album *L'Estampe originale* (Delteil, state 3).
Colls: Art Institute of Chicago (laid paper, signed "AR"); Bibliothèque Nationale (copy of *L'Estampe originale*, plus two separate impressions: both laid paper, one signed "AR"); British Museum; Metropolitan Museum of Art (*L'Estampe originale*); Musée Rodin; National Museum of Western Art, Tokyo; Philadelphia Museum of Art (China paper); Stanford University Museum of Art (*L'Estampe originale*); The Grunwald Center for the Graphic Arts, University of California, Los Angeles.

29   Musée Rodin.
Impression of state 4 with spots and no margins. Probably impression catalogued by Delteil as a new state "with spots . . . especially one at bottom right" (Delteil, state 4) and printed after the impressions for *L'Estampe originale*. Delteil's state 5 and final state follows this and is described as having the spots removed and plate very worn. However, a very late, worn impression (Fig. 30) has most spots and scratches (though much lighter), with the exception of the large spot an inch from bottom right. While the large spot may have been removed, other spots and scratches disappear and reappear on late impressions depending on how the plate was inked and wiped. Thus no significant changes in the image allow cataloguing of additional states after state 4, and only quality distinctions can be made depending on how worn the plate is.

30   National Museum of Western Art, Tokyo.
Late, worn impression of state 4 with spots and no margins.

Three different views of the head dramatically confront each other and the viewer in the drypoint *Henri Becque* (Fig. 25). The drypoint was copied from the terra-cotta bust (see Fig. 31 for bronze version), perhaps with the aid of an intermediary drawing. Chronologies assign the bust to the year 1883 or 1886,[1] and Rodin dates the drypoint after the bust to 1887 in his letter to M. Bourcard. In the drypoint the modeling of the forehand, protruding brow line, bow tie, chest and shoulder silhouette all correspond to the terra-cotta bust. A few reverse details are also discernible, such as Becque's slightly parted and ruffled hair which appears on the left in the bust and on the right in the print.

In the drypoint, the three different views of the bust, two of them slightly askew from strict left and right profiles, and a third nearly full front view in the center, appear staged like the three Horatii of David. The theatrical composition may be intentional as Henri Becque (1837–1900), a close friend of Rodin, was a well-known dramatist and restorer of great realistic comedy. A copy of his masterpiece, *Les Corbeaux*, written in 1882, along with *Honnêtes Femmes* are in Rodin's library with dedications to the sculptor.[2]

The playwright was among the distinguished writers, artists, and statesmen, including J.-P. Laurens, Legros, Dalou, Antonin Proust, and Victor Hugo, whose portraits Rodin made in the early 1880's when he began his series of busts of famous men and women.[3] Typical of Rodin's portrait sculpture, the head is frontal and the seriously intent expression is concentrated in the furrowed brow, taut cheek

25

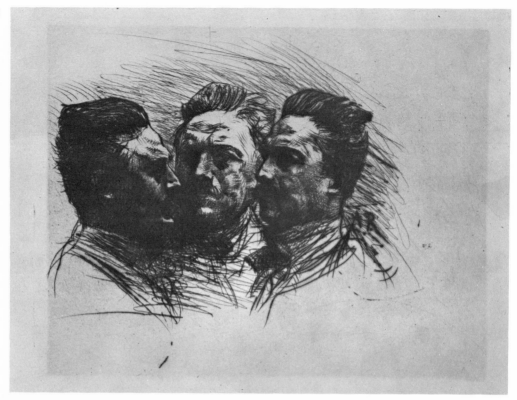

26

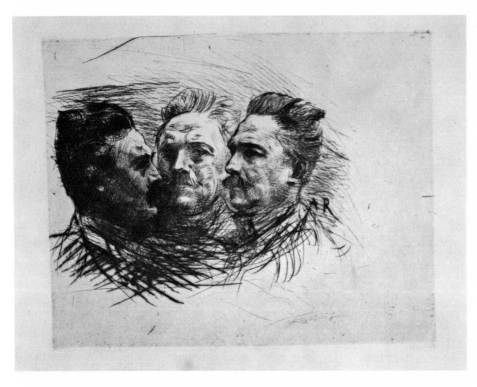

29

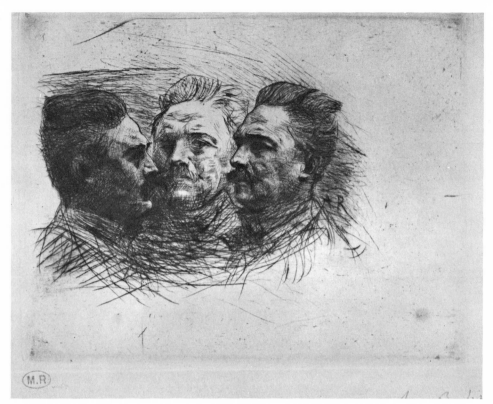

30

muscles and distant gaze. To Rodin the chest silhouette of these busts was an expressive detail to be treated not as a formula but meshed creatively with the attitude of the head. For the three drypoint compositions after the sculpture busts, three divergent chest silhouettes were used as a point of departure. The rough edge of Becque's coat in the sculpture was translated into long, slashing strokes in the drypoint, while the Victor Hugo drypoint follows a smoother silhouette of the coat and the Antonin Proust ends with the sharp, curved edge of the bust.

In the first state of *Henri Becque*, the merging of figure and ground is carefully controlled as the long, slashed lines at the base of the heads describe a series of firm shoulder and chest profiles corresponding to the silhouette of the terracotta bust. The interwoven base lines echoed by lighter swirling scratches behind, both augmented in state 2 (Fig. 26), unify the three heads and suggest a movement or rotation of the bust while creating a miasma from which the heads enigmatically emerge. The coalescing of the figure with ground is also treated in the low relief to nearly three-dimensional sculpture on the *Gates of Hell* and in single sculptures like *Thought* (1886) where a head emerges from rough marble. In the third and fourth states of *Henri Becque* (Figs. 27 and 28), the base lines are extended and become successively more diffuse as Rodin attempted to revitalize a worn plate with a new burr without greatly disturbing the delicate facial modeling which also grows increasingly lighter.

1. While most chronologies date the bust 1886, Cladel and Grappe give the date 1883 (Cladel, *Rodin*, 199; Grappe, no. 100).

2. Grappe, no. 100.

3. See Elsen, *Rodin*, 107–131.

RELATED SCULPTURE

31   *Henri Becque*. 1907 (?). Bronze. (Large terra cotta. 1883–1886). H. 6 in. (15.2 cm.). Philadelphia Museum of Art.

REPRODUCTIONS (in Rodin's lifetime)

L'Art et les Artistes, 1905, 30; and 1914, 89 (state 3 reproduced).

Catalogue des Estampes Modernes Composant la Collection Roger Marx, opp. 74 (listed as state 1, but is state 2).

Cladel, *Auguste Rodin*, opp. 148.

Delteil, no. 9.

Les Maîtres Artistes, between 292 and 293.

Marx, *Les Pointes Sèches de Rodin*, 12.

Sparrow, "Auguste Rodin's Dry-Point Engravings," 91.

31

VIII. Victor Hugo, de Trois Quarts (Victor Hugo, Three-Quarters View). 1885.

9 x 7 in. (22.9 x 17.8 cm.) *States 1–3.*
8⅝ x 5-15/16 in. (21.9 x 15 cm.) *States 4–8.*

State One
32   The Art Institute of Chicago (ivory laid paper).
Inscribed *"hommage à notre grand artiste à Roll / Rodin."*
Before four vertical lines added on principal head to collar at left above initials "AR;" before new work on beard of lower head.
Coll: National Gallery of Art, Washington (laid paper; inscribed in sepia ink *"à mon cher cousin Henri Chefter"*).

State Two
33   Bibliothèque Nationale (laid paper).
Inscribed *"A mon vieux ami et maître Legros / A Rodin."*
Four vertical lines added on principal head to collar at left above initials "AR" and edge of beard redefined on left; beard of lower head extended and darkened. Measurements of the Bibliothèque Nationale impression differ slightly: 8⅞ x 6-15/16 in. (22.5 x 17.6 cm.).
Colls: British Museum; Daniel Guerin, private collection, Paris (signed "Auguste Rodin"); Metropolitan Museum of Art (wove paper, watermark "MBM"); Musée du Louvre (inscribed *"A Monsieur Dreyfus hommage du sculpteur A Rodin"*).

State Three
34   The Minneapolis Institute of Arts, gift of Phillip W. Pillsbury (cream laid paper).
Inscribed *"Rodin / Victor Hugo de ¾."*
Area of coat of principal head greatly enlarged, covering initials "AR" on collar at left and adding deep black tone under the white beard; signature "A Rodin" added at right and printed backward; new lines added to back of neck, new burr added in spots to the forehead.
Coll: Musée Rodin.

State Four
35   National Gallery of Art, Washington, Rosenwald Collection.
No change in image, thin rectangular frame line drawn around image; width of plate reduced to 5-15/16 in., height of plate not cut down but frame line reduces height of background area; longest shoulder line of lower head crosses over bottom frame line.
Coll: Boston Museum of Fine Arts (China paper).

State Five
36   National Gallery of Art, Washington, Rosenwald Collection.
Inscribed *"A Monsieur Leopold Hugo / hommage du sculpteur / A Rodin."*
Lower head and lower dotted trial heads erased; light frame line of state 4 erased and clearer frame line added; title "VICTOR HUGO" printed at center below head; at bottom frame line name of periodical, "L'Artiste," added to left and printer, "Imp. L. Eudes," to right; printed in black ink on laid paper and included as an original print in *L'Artiste*, February 1885, opp. 156 (index of issue, p. 483, states, *"Victor Hugo, pointe sèche par le sculpteur A. Rodin"*).
Colls: Bibliothèque Nationale; Philadelphia Museum of Art.

32

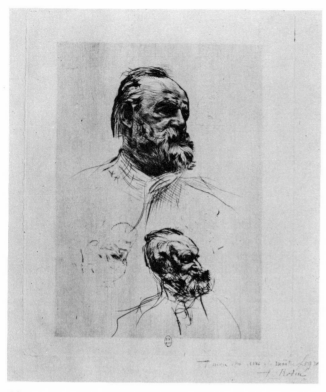

33

34

35

36

State Six

37   The Fine Arts Museums of San Francisco (moderately thick wove paper).

Same as state 5 with title "VICTOR HUGO" but name of periodical and printer are erased; printed in black ink and published as an original print in Geffroy, "Le Statuaire Rodin," *Les Lettres et les Arts*, September 1889, opp. 302 (index of issue states, "*Portrait de Victor Hugo, eau-forte de M. Rodin en regard de la page 302*"); printed in dark brown ink and included as an original print in the same article published as a separate pamphlet in Geffroy, *Le Statuaire Rodin* (see *Bibliography*).
Colls: Bibliothèque Nationale; British Museum; Philadelphia Museum of Art.

State Seven

38   Musée Rodin.
Signed "A Rodin."
No changes except that the title "VICTOR HUGO" is erased. The Musée Rodin also possesses a proof of this state with unique inking in which the plate is wiped clean of ink except for the head and the area very close to it.
Colls: Kestner Museum, Hannover; National Museum of Western Art, Tokyo.

State Eight

39   Musée Rodin.
Lines worn and head appears very light; entire plate toned with delicate scratches; small putto facing forward added to lower left (Delteil says putto added in 1900 and that there were some proofs of putto alone).
Coll: Stadtköln, Wallraf-Richartz Museum.

Differences in the drypoints *Victor Hugo, Three-Quarters View* (Fig. 32) and *Victor Hugo, Front View* (Fig. 46) correspond to two aspects which Rodin saw in the great writer's physiognomy: "Hugo had the air of a Hercules; belonged to a great race. Something of a tiger, or an old lion. He had an immense animal nature. His eyes were especially beautiful and the most striking thing about him."[1] The first drypoint, the *Three-Quarters View*, emphasizes Hugo's animal nature with the mountainous triangularity of the shoulders, the disordered lion-like hair, the craggy lumps across his forehead, and the claw-like lines extended from the neck of the lower head. In the second, *Front View*, the hair is smoothed, the bristled beard more orderly, the coat flatter, less expansive and tighter to the neck. Nothing draws attention from the

37

38

39

frontal view of the soft, deep velvety eye sockets which Rodin shows, as he describes them, as the most striking and beautiful feature.

Both views are extraordinary, but the *Three-Quarters View* is more expressive of the powerful initial impression of the great man while the *Front View* shows a growing refinement of conception and technique. Rodin's first attempts at placing and determining the scale of the heads in the *Three-Quarters View* can be seen from the two small dotted trial heads, while in the *Front View* Rodin confidently balanced the composition without trial sketches. Further, in state 1 of the *Front View*, Rodin gouged a concise row of deep black ridges along the jacket opening at the neck, producing a vibrant triangular accent which offsets the face and white beard, an effect he achieved in state 3 of *Three-Quarters View* (Fig. 34) after reworking the plate with multiple hachure.

Besides the stylistic criteria for dating the *Victor Hugo, Three-Quarters View* first, state 5 (Fig. 36) of this view was published in *l'Artiste* in February 1885 so that the first four states most likely date to the first two months of 1885, although the *Three-Quarters View* could possibly have been done some months previously in 1884 when the bronze bust of Victor Hugo was executed and shown at the Salon.[2] The second and more dignified *Front View* appears to have been executed during 1885, perhaps in response to Hugo's death. Rodin assigns the date 1885 to both drypoints "*Victor Hugo ¾ à droite*" and "*Victor Hugo de face*," his titles listed in his 1903 letter to M. Bourcard. Moreover, the inscription "*A Monsieur Lucas / hommage respectueux / Rodin / Paris 8 Octobre 1887*" written on one impression of *Victor Hugo, Front View*, state 2, gives a terminus date for that state of the drypoint.[3]

When Rodin first met Victor Hugo in 1883, two years before the writer's death at eighty-two, he refused to allow Rodin sittings for a bust. While details of the story of Rodin's work on the bust vary, the accounts generally follow the two earliest given by sculptor and art critic T. H. Bartlett in 1888[4] and by the famous writer Edmond de Goncourt, based on a visit with Rodin in December 1886:

> He went on for a long time about his bust of Hugo, who did not pose but who let him come to him as often as he wished. He made a stack of sketches of the great poet—I think sixty—from the right, the left, and above, almost all foreshortened, in attitudes of reading or meditation, sketches from which he was obliged to make the bust.[5]

Small pencil and pen drawings in a private collection in Paris (Figs. 40 and 41), at the Musée Rodin (Fig. 42; Fig. 43; Fig. 44; MR 2109 and MR 2110) and reproduced in a biography of Rodin in 1899[6] correspond to those described by witnesses as the sketches made quickly on simple note pad paper showing Victor Hugo concentrating at work or engaged in daily affairs. While accounts differ as to whether Rodin set up his stand to model the clay bust from the veranda or returned home to work,[7] he still could not follow his customary procedure of arduously comparing his model's head profile by profile with the clay bust. The sketches, however, helped him note down these observations from every angle. In one drawing which explores the three-quarters view (Fig. 40) adapted in the first drypoint, Rodin went over the initial lines with heavy black strokes to stress certain profiles and added white gouache to help him envision the highlights. The composition of the drawing showing two heads on one sheet, though done here for expediency, was carried over to both Hugo drypoints and recurs frequently in Rodin's portrait drawings (Fig. 167) and drypoints as late as his last drypoint (Fig. 73) of 1916.

Contrary to all accounts, the large main heads of the two drypoints were not done from the quick sketches made at Victor Hugo's home but were either copied directly from the bronze bust of Hugo dated 1884 (Fig. 45), or from an intermediary drawing after the bronze. The two small, dotted trial heads in the *Three-Quarters View* may have been made by punching needle points through the paper; this may also have been the method of transfer from a drawing for the main head since some dotted lines show through where the burr is worn in late impressions. The small dotted heads may also demonstrate Rodin's method of tentatively dotting out a contour directly on the plate as a guide for more fluid lines.[8]

The strongest evidence for the assertion that the principal heads in both drypoints were copied from the bronze bust is that the line of Hugo's coat, which closes to the right in the bronze, was copied exactly as observed in the bust and is reversed in the print.[9] In the *Front View* all of the facial modeling also appears reversed, the exact shape of the circles under the eyes, the crevices in the cheeks, the narrow diagonal trough at the edge of one side of the beard, etc. Furthermore, the two profiles of Hugo's beard are dramatically different when seen in a three-quarters view of the bust (Fig. 45). The bushy profile of the beard, which sweeps out toward the observer's left in the bust, appears exactly reversed in the print, making it clear that Rodin worked from the right view of the bust for his drypoint *Three-Quarters View*. It also appears that Rodin looked up at the bust set on a table or stand when working on the plates or preparatory drawings as the viewpoint of both drypoints is from below. The subject appears slightly elevated from this vantage point, adding a sense of dignity not apparent in Alphonse Legros' engraving of *Victor Hugo* as a tired octo-genarian.[10] In Rodin's preparatory drawings, he had also shown the old sunken cheeks and slack muscles around the eyes which Legros records in his engraving, but in Rodin's bust and drypoints the old face is strengthened and ennobled. Although both artists convey the force of Victor Hugo's mind in concentration, the dynamic structure of the sculptural modeling in Rodin's drypoint enhances the feeling of mystery and power of the great writer.

1. T. H. Bartlett, "Auguste Rodin, Sculptor," in Elsen (ed.), *Auguste Rodin, Readings on His Life and Work*, 56.
2. Salon des Artistes Françaises, *Bust of Victor Hugo*, bronze, no. 3862.
3. The drypoint is on indefinite loan to The Baltimore Museum of Art.
4. Bartlett, "Auguste Rodin, Sculptor," 55–56.
5. Goncourt, *Journal des Goncourt*, 227, Thursday, December 29, 1887.
6. Maillard, *Auguste Rodin, Statuaire*, 9, 12, 18, 87, 97, 99, 100, 101, 102.
7. Bartlett ("Auguste Rodin, Sculptor," 55) says that Rodin worked on the bust from the veranda of Victor Hugo's apartment. Judith Cladel agrees with this account (Cladel, *Rodin: The Man and His Art*, 302). C. Lawton, however, says that Rodin "hurried home" to work on the bust (Lawton, *The Life and Work of Auguste Rodin*, 84). Other accounts of Rodin's work on the bust appear in Dujardin-Beaumetz, "Rodin's Reflections on Art," in Elsen (ed.), *Auguste Rodin, Readings on His Life and Work*, 169–170; Bergerat, *Souvenirs d'un enfant de Paris*, 254–255; Gsell, *Art by Auguste Rodin*, 142–146.
8. The drawing sources and methods of constructing the two small, secondary heads included at the bottom of both drypoints are too varied to permit interpretation.
9. The left to right closing of Victor Hugo's coat in the bronze bust is actually incorrect according to men's fashion of the period. This may be a clue to Rodin's use of photographs, engravings or other sources as an aid in modeling the bust.
10. Reproduced in *The Studio*, January 1903, 246. Etching, c. 1878, state 1, 5⅞ x 4⅜ in. (22.5 x 11 cm.).

RELATED DRAWINGS

40 *Victor Hugo, Three-Quarters View, Two Heads on One Sheet.* 1884. Pen and ink, gray wash, white gouache. 4¼ x 3¾ in. (10.8 x 9.5 cm.) [measurement of mat opening]. Signed "Rodin." Location unknown; formerly Daniel Guerin, private collection, Paris.

41 *Victor Hugo, Front View.* 1884. Charcoal, flesh tone wash. 3⅝ x 3 in. (9.2 x 7.6 cm.). Daniel Guerin, private collection, Paris.

42 *Victor Hugo, Front View and Profile.* 1884. Pen and ink. 3⅛ x 5½ in. (8 x 13 cm.). MR 2166.

43 *Victor Hugo, Front View.* 1884. Pencil, gray wash, white gouache. 6 x 4 in. (15.2 x 10.2 cm.). MR 5356.

44 *Victor Hugo in Profile, on Sheet with Nude Male Figure.* 1884. Pen and ink. 6 x 5¼ in. (15.2 x 13.3 cm.). Signed "Aug Rodin." MR 5355.

40

41

42

RELATED SCULPTURE

45 *Victor Hugo.* 1884. Bronze. 16⅞ in. (42.9 cm.). The Fine Arts Museums of San Francisco.

RELATED DRAWINGS NOT REPRODUCED
Victor Hugo. 1884. Pencil. 3-15/16 x 2 in. (10 x 5 cm.).
MR 2109 (matted together with MR 1966, 2110, 5305).
Victor Hugo. 1884. Pencil. 4¼ x 2½ in. (10.8 x 6.4 cm.).
MR 2110 (matted together with MR 1966, 2109, 5305).

REPRODUCTIONS (in Rodin's lifetime)
L'Art et les Artistes, 1905, 29; 1914, 85 (state 2).
Catalogue des Estampes Modernes Composant la Collection Roger Marx, no. 1082 (state 3).
Cladel, *Auguste Rodin,* opp. 146.
Delteil, no. 6.
Les Maîtres Artistes, between 292 and 293 (state 8).
Marx, "Auguste Rodin," 194 (state 2).
Marx, *Les Pointes Sèches de Rodin,* 7 (state 5).
Sparrow, "Auguste Rodin's Dry-Point Engravings," 90 (state 2), 91 (state with small head erased).

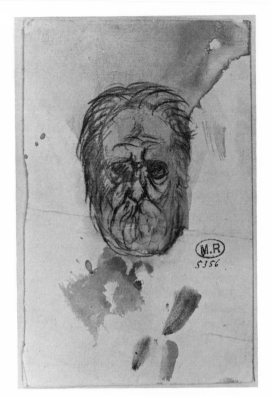

43

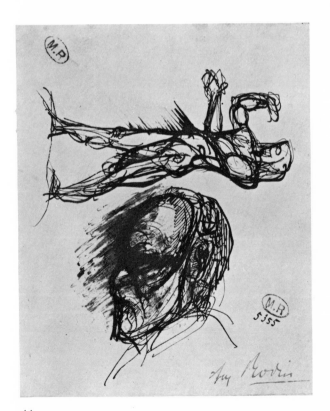

44

45 (*See Appendix A, p. 140*)

IX. Victor Hugo, de Face (Victor Hugo, Front View). 1885.
8 7/8 x 6 7/8 in. (22.5 x 17.5 cm.) *States 1–4.*
8 7/8 x 6 1/4 in. (22.5 x 15.9 cm.) *States 5–9.*

46

State One
46   Location unknown. Reproduced from Delteil.
Before curve of back of lower head is rounded out with
new modeling.

State Two
47   British Museum.
Inscribed "*à mon ami E. V. Henley / A Rodin.*"
New modeling rounds out back of lower head and lines
are added to side of head.
Colls: The Baltimore Museum of Art; Daniel Guerin, private collection, Paris (signed "Auguste Rodin"); Metropolitan Museum of Art (laid paper); Musée Rodin (signed
"Aug Rodin"); National Gallery of Art, Washington
(signed "Rodin").   .

State Three
48   Private collection, Oxford; formerly P. & D. Colnaghi
& Co., Ltd., London.
Inscribed "*A mon ami Felicien Rops / A Rodin.*"
Initials "AR" added at left to coat; new modeling to front of
coat increases black area under chin; a button added to coat;
new burr accentuates shading in eyes and beard; before
series of short horizontal lines added across opening of coat
and before several lines added to both shoulders (not catalogued by Delteil).
Coll: Private collection, Boston; formerly R. M. Light &
Company, Inc., Boston.

State Four
49   National Gallery of Art, Washington, Rosenwald
Collection.
Inscribed "*Hommage du Sculpteur/ à Monsieur Leopold Hugo/
Rodin.*"
Series of short horizontal lines drawn across opening of
coat; two small diagonal lines added to top of shoulder at
right; two long diagonal lines added at bottom of series of
lines describing shoulder at left (Delteil, state 3). The
Musée Rodin has a proof of state 4 with notations for printing state 5. Notations include pencil guidelines for new
margins, reduction of plate size, beveling of edges, as well
as several inscriptions: "*15 les biseaux compris,*" "*bon à tirer
30 épr. 1/4 col. en deux tons suivant modèle avant de couper le
cuivre puis 60 1/8 col. cuivre coupé Hollande jaune,*" plus one

47

illegible inscription. Before the plate was to be cut down
30 impressions were to be pulled, 15 after the plate was
beveled.
Colls (state 4 before plate beveled): Boston Museum of
Fine Arts (laid paper, inscribed "*A mon sincere ami un grand
peintre / Roll / A Rodin*"); British Museum (inscribed "*A M.
Colvin / Conservateur en / Estampes au British Museum / hommage
Colvin A Rodin*"); The Fine Arts Museums of San Francisco
(laid paper, watermark "Arches"); Philadelphia Museum
of Art (Japan paper, acc. no. 53-119-5); Victoria and Albert
Museum.
Colls (state 4 with plate beveled): Cantor, Fitzgerald Art
Foundation (signed "A Rodin"); Fogg Art Museum (wove
paper); Philadelphia Museum of Art (wove paper, acc. no.
F29-7-208); Rhode Island School of Design Museum of
Art; Stadtköln, Wallraf-Richartz Museum (thin Japan
paper).

State Five
50   Museum of Fine Arts, Boston, bequest of Lee M. Friedman (acc. no. 58.140).
No change in image, width of plate cut down to 6¼ in.
(15.9 cm.) (Delteil, state 4); printed in black ink and published as an original print in deluxe edition of *Gazette des
Beaux-Arts*, March 1889; probably an edition of sixty, see
inscription on proof of state 4.
Colls: Boston Museum of Fine Arts, second impression
(acc. no. 50.3272); Staatliche Museum, Berlin.

State Six
51   Philadelphia Museum of Art (print still in text).
No change in image; words added at center below image:
"VICTOR HUGO/ *Etude à la pointe sèche par M. A.
Rodin.*", at left: "Gazette des Beaux-Arts" and at right:
"Imp. A. Clement Paris" (Delteil, state 5); printed in black
ink on laid paper with watermark "Arches" and included
as an original print in *Gazette des Beaux-Arts*, March 1889,
ordinary edition, opp. 238 (index says, "*Victor Hugo, étude
à la pointe sèche par M. A. Rodin; gravure tirée hors texte*").
Colls: The Fine Arts Museums of San Francisco (letters
removed); Frick Art Reference Library, New York City
(print still in text); Metropolitan Museum of Art Library
(print still in text); The Minneapolis Institute of Arts;
Musée Rodin.

State Seven
52   Philadelphia Museum of Art (print still in text).
No change in image; words of state 6 erased and new words
added at center: "Rodin sc. / VICTOR HUGO" (Delteil,

48

49

50

VICTOR HUGO
Étude à la pointe sèche par M. A. Rodin

51

Rodin del
VICTOR HUGO

52

M.R

53

state 7); printed in black ink and included as an original print in Marx, *Les Pointes Sèches de Rodin*, frontispiece. The burr is inexplicably richer than in state 6; possibly Roger Marx bought an edition for his book of 1902 before state 6 was printed in 1889.
Colls: Musée Rodin; University of Glasgow.

State Eight
53   Musée Rodin.
Signed "A. Rodin."
No change in image; letters below inked area erased from previous state; initials "AR" erased (not catalogued by Delteil as separate state; Delteil says in some impressions initials "AR" not inked).
Coll: National Museum of Western Art, Tokyo.

State Nine
54   Philadelphia Museum of Art, given by Jules Mastbaum.
Small putto turned and walking left added lower left corner; plate worn (Delteil lists as state 6 and second to last state, but it is doubtful that initials "AR" would disappear in state with putto and reappear a state later; furthermore, cross-hatching behind putto is drawn across a long diagonal scratch present in all previous states—the scratch line would have been affected if putto were erased; worn condition of plate also indicates last state).
Colls: British Museum; Musée Rodin; Staatliche Museum, Berlin.

For discussion and related drawings and sculpture, refer to no. VIII.

REPRODUCTIONS (in Rodin's lifetime)
Catalogue des Estampes Modernes Composant la Collection Roger Marx, no. 1083 (the rare state 3).
Cladel, *Auguste Rodin*, opp. 146.
Delteil, no. 7.
La Revue des Beaux-Arts et des Lettres, 19.
Les Maîtres Artistes, between 292 and 293 (state 8).
Maillard, *Auguste Rodin, Statuaire*, 144 (state 1).
Sparrow, "Auguste Rodin's Dry-Point Engravings," 93 (an excellent impression of the rare state 2 with a great deal of burr, as well as a late impression).

54

X. Antonin Proust. 1884-1888.
9⅜ x 7 in. (23.8 x 17.9 cm.) *States 1–5.*
8 x 5½ in. (20.4 x 14 cm.) *States 6–7.*

State One
55   The Art Institute of Chicago (cream laid paper).
Before lines of neck extended into chest.
Coll: Musée Rodin.

State Two
56   National Gallery of Art, Washington, Rosenwald
Collection.
Lines of neck continued into clavicle and chest following
silhouette of sculpture bust; extensive work on head to
reinforce lines, add new modeling and create a heavy burr.
Coll: Musée Rodin.

State Three
57   British Museum.
Signed "A Rodin."
Numerous lines added to hair between more widely spaced
dark lines of state 2; line of back of head reinforced along
curls and just below on neck; new modeling, notably a
series of diagonal lines at throat and back of neck, lines drawn
from hairline at top of forehead back into hair, and small
dark cross-hatched patches on eyebrow and just below
bridge of nose.

State Four
58   Musée Rodin.
Curved line drawn just behind ear; tiny additions to model-
ing such as series of short hooked lines at throat and in
beard halfway between earlobe and mustache; burr worn;
little contrast and overall gray tonality; plate beveled.
Colls: Bibliothèque Nationale; Cleveland Museum of Art;
Maryland Institute College of Art, on indefinite loan to
The Baltimore Museum of Art; Minneapolis Institute of
Arts (cream laid paper); National Gallery of Art, Washing-
ton (inscribed "*à mon ami Mulhem (?) A Rodin*"); National
Museum of Western Art, Tokyo (signed "Aug Rodin");
Princeton University Art Museum; Toledo Museum of Art.

55

56

59 Musée Rodin, MR 5305.
A proof of state 4 with changes for state 5. Pen and ink
drawn over the drypoint; measuring 5⅝ x 4⅜ in. (14.3 x
11.1 cm.).

State Five
60 Metropolitan Museum of Art Library (still in text).
Ear lobe narrowed by vertical lines; new lines in hair near
forehead form distinctive triangular shape; series of curved
horizontal lines sweep across chin in beard; other small
additions to modeling. Printed in black ink and included as
an original print in Marx, "Auguste Rodin," opp. 190; on
sheet bottom left written, "AUGUSTE RODIN, ANTONIN
PROUST ORIGINALRADIERUNG PAN III 3."
Colls: Art Institute of Chicago (cream wove paper); Bibliothèque Nationale (still in text); Boston Museum of Fine
Arts (wove paper); British Museum; Cantor, Fitzgerald
Art Foundation; Kestner Museum, Hannover; National
Gallery of Art, Washington; New York Public Library
(still in text); Princeton University Art Museum (inscribed
"*A Monsieur Zelkern*"); Staatliche Kunstsammlungen,
Dresden; Stadtköln, Wallraf-Richartz Museum.

57

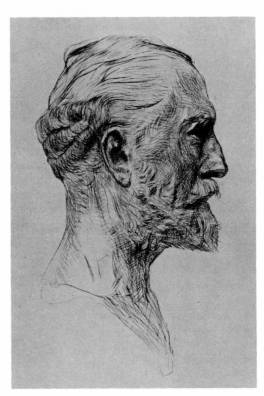

58

59

60

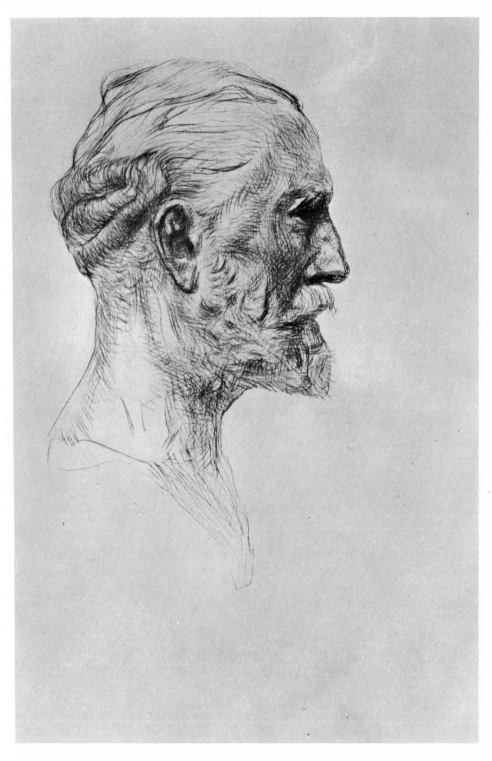

61

ANTONIN PROUST

62

State Six

61   Philadelphia Museum of Art Library (still in text of deluxe edition).

No change in image; plate size reduced; printed in dark brown ink on wove paper and included as an original print in the deluxe edition of Maillard, *Auguste Rodin, Statuaire*. Deluxe edition numbered 1 to 60, with abbreviation "N°" on colophon but number itself sometimes omitted; text paper Japan paper with a second suite of most prints on China paper and a few such as the *Antonin Proust* on *vèlin de Rives* (wove); second print of *Antonin Proust* in deluxe edition is of state 7.

State Seven

62   Philadelphia Museum of Art Library (still in text of deluxe edition).

No change in image; letters "ANTONIN PROUST" added at bottom center; printed in red-brown ink on wove paper and included as an original print in *both* deluxe edition and ordinary edition of Maillard, *Auguste Rodin, Statuaire*; page listing *hors texte* prints in both deluxe and ordinary edition notes "ANTONIN PROUST (*pointe sèche de Rodin*)"; ordinary edition omits the abbreviation "N°" from the colophon.
Colls: Beinecke Rare Book and Manuscript Library, Yale University (ordinary edition); The Fine Arts Museums of

San Francisco; Albert Elsen, private collection, Palo Alto (ordinary edition); Fogg Art Museum Library (ordinary edition); Frick Art Reference Library, New York (ordinary edition); New York Public Library (ordinary edition).

Two letters from Antonin Proust to Rodin postponing sittings establish that Rodin was working on the terra-cotta bust in March and April 1884.[1] The drypoint may date to that year or the year following when a bronze cast of the bust was exhibited at the 1885 Salon. Rodin, however, assigns the drypoint to the year 1888 in his letter to M. Bourcard, listing it as the last of the three drypoint portraits. Like the other three drypoint portraits of Henri Becque and the two views of Victor Hugo, the *Antonin Proust* (Fig. 55) was executed after the sculpture bust (Fig. 63) and reverses the view of the bust that it was copied from. The *Antonin Proust* drypoint carefully duplicates the bust's right profile view with its three rows of curls, flamboyant sweep of the beard, and undercut cowlicks on the forehead and top of the head; these details differ markedly from the bust's left profile view.

In state 1 of the drypoint (Fig. 55), the rendering stops at the neck and does not continue into the chest as in the bust, which results in a more immediate impression of the man. In state 2 (Fig. 56), Rodin reinforced contour lines, added new modeling and extended the neck lines into the sharp, oval silhouette of the bare chest so that the drypoint more clearly resembles the bust. To a contemporary of Rodin, the connection between the drypoint and the sculpture was obvious: "When printed in warm sepia, it [the drypoint] looks like a bronze medallion."[2] Rodin no doubt intended to create this impression as both the bust and drypoint, states 2 through 7, present Antonin Proust as a noble Roman statesman. His lips are drawn and slightly parted as if he were speaking, his eyes are gazing into the future, and the silhouette of his bare chest follows the style of a Roman bust.

Antonin Proust (1832–1905) was a French politician, *Député d'Union républicaine* from 1876–1896, concerned with foreign affairs and the fine arts and at one time the Minister of Fine Arts. An official title by which Rodin knew him, printed on an undated calling card among Rodin's papers, was "*Député President de l'Union Centrale des Arts Décoratifs.*"[3] He was also a friend and admirer of the sculptor and instrumental in his receiving the Cross of the Chevalier of the Legion of Honor in 1888.[4]

The delicacy of touch, sense of distance implicit in a strict profile view, and careful control of details of hair and beard

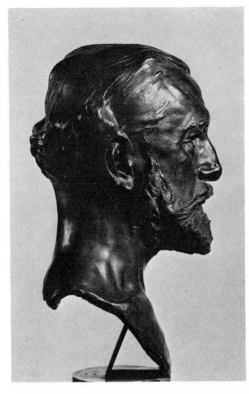

63

which remain close to a sharp delineation of silhouette, all inspire respect and a refined sense of dignity. In states 3 (Fig. 57) and 4 (Fig. 58) of the drypoint, added lines produce some new burr but do not bring back the more spontaneous and vibrant modeling of state 2. Similarly, a proof of state 4 (Fig. 59) with pen notations for changes in state 5 indicates that Rodin intended to enliven the worn plate with new burr and forceful, sweeping lines, changes which were greatly muted when ultimately transposed onto the copper plate.

1. Letter from Antonin Proust to Rodin, Sunday, March 23, 1884. Musée Rodin archives, Proust folder. "*Mon cher Maître / Voulez vous que nous remettions à mercredi notre séance. Je suis pris jusque là par des . . .(?) / Cordialement à vous / Antonin Proust / le dimanche 23 mars 1884.*" Second letter from Antonin Proust to Rodin, Tuesday, April 10, 1884 on letterhead "*Chambre des Députés.*" Musée Rodin archives, Proust folder. "*Mon cher Maître / Me voici encore pris ce matin par une réunion imprévue que a lieu au Louvre à la Salle des Etats dans le but de préparer l'exposition des chansons de la commune. J'espérais pouvoir me dispenser d'assister à cette réunion mais il faut paraît-il que je renonce à cette espérance. J'irai très certainement vous voir demain pour convenir d'une séance prochaine. / Cordialement à vous / Antonin Proust / le jeudi matin 10 avril 1884.*"
2. Lawton, *The Life and Work of Auguste Rodin*, 100.
3. Musée Rodin archives, Proust folder.
4. T. H. Bartlett, "Auguste Rodin, Sculptor," in Elsen (ed.), *Auguste Rodin, Readings on His Life and Work*, 109.

RELATED SCULPTURE
63   *Antonin Proust.* 1884–1885. Bronze. H. 16¼ in. (41.3 cm.). Fogg Art Museum, bequest of Grenville L. Winthrop.

REPRODUCTIONS (in Rodin's lifetime)
Cladel, *Auguste Rodin*, opp. 150.
Delteil, no. 10.
Grautoff, *Rodin*, 104 (state 4).
Marx, *Les Pointes Sèches de Rodin*, 10.
Sparrow, "Auguste Rodin's Dry-Point Engravings," 92.

XI. Le Centaure Mourant
(The Dying Centaur). 1886-1889.
7¼ x 9¼ in. (18.4 x 23.5 cm.)

Unique State
64   Private collection, Zurich; formerly collection of
August Laube, Zurich.
Signed three times in pen, "A Rodin."
Verso: *Tomb Monument*. 1886–1889. Charcoal.

The drypoint *The Dying Centaur* (Fig. 64), a strange composition of a centaur whose human upper body bends
backward while his animal body gallops forward, was not
known to Delteil and remained undiscovered until Claude
Roger-Marx saw it in a Swiss sales catalogue in 1926.[1] The
centaur's body in the drypoint appears to have been taken
from the left profile view of the horse in the equestrian
Monument to General Lynch dated 1886 (Fig. 67), the drypoint reversing the pose of the sculpture. The horse's
charge, taken from the monument, contrasts with a human
body tortuously doubled backward in the drypoint, its
head and arms dangling limply, dramatizing the well-
known classical theme of the conflict between man's
animal and human nature.

The sculptures of a *Centauress* of 1889 and a centaur
depicted on the left bas relief of the *Gates of Hell* symbolize,
like the groups of tormented human figures in the *Gates*,
different aspects of the agony of existence. The centaur in
the drypoint has a similar connotation of psychological torment which is more likely the cause of its suffering than
any mortal wounds, particularly since it is not clear if Rodin
intended to show the centaur dying or if he actually titled
it "Dying Centaur." When Rodin showed a centaur in
death throes in a related drawing (Fig. 65) it was halted in
flight, its body shot with arrows and contracted in pain. In
another drawing of a wounded centaur (Fig. 66), Rodin
showed the creature bending forward to stop the blood
flowing from its injured front leg, and he wrote on the
drawing, "Bandaging his Wound" ("*Bandant sa Blessure*").

In the drypoint *The Dying Centaur*, the smooth, fine modeling along the centaur's body, also used on the vase in the
drypoint *Amphora* (Fig. 24), contrasts with more freely
drawn contour lines, some of which are reinforced with pen
and ink to accent features like the grotesquely contorted
face. The drypoint composition was reproduced as the
frontispiece for the book *Auguste Rodin, Statuaire* by Léon
Riotor, published in 1900.

1. Roger-Marx, "Engravings by Sculptors in France," 155. *Une Collection Merveilleuse des Eaux-Fortes, Lithographies et Clichés-Verres des Grands Maîtres Françaises du XIX siècle*, H. Gilhofer and H. Ranschburg Ltd., Lucerne, Vente aux Enchères à Lucerne, June 8–9, 1926, 36, no. 392 illustrated. I would like to thank Dr. Margret Stuffman of the Städelsches Kunstinstitut for helping me locate *The Dying Centaur* and Mr. August Laube for providing me with photographs.

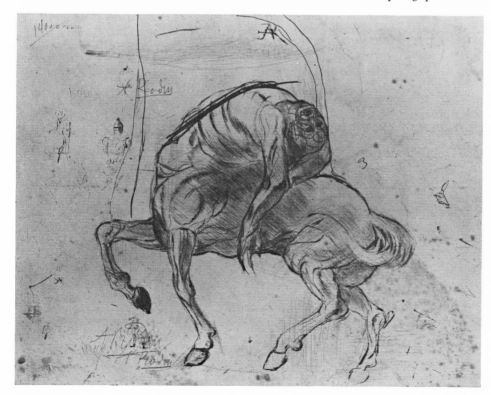

64

67

RELATED DRAWINGS

65   *Centaur Shot with Arrows*. 1886–1889. Brown pen and ink. 4 7/8 x 5 1/4 in. (12.4 x 13.3 cm.). MR 1896.

66   *Centaur Bandaging his Wound*. 1886–1889. Pencil, pen and ink on graph paper. 4 7/8 x 5-15/16 in. (12.4 x 15 cm.). MR 1888.

RELATED SCULPTURE

67   *Study for Equestrian Statue of General Lynch*. 1886. Plaster. H. 17 3/4 in. (45 cm.). Musée Rodin.

RELATED DRAWINGS NOT REPRODUCED

Centaur. 1880–1889. Pen and ink. 5 3/4 x 7 1/2 in. (14.5 x 19.1 cm.). Verso of drawing *Le Sabbat*. The Art Institute of Chicago.

RELATED SCULPTURE NOT REPRODUCED

Centauress. c. 1889. Bronze. H. 15 3/4 in. (40 cm.). Musée Rodin. Reproduced in *Rodin: Sculpture and Drawings*, an exhibition organized by the Arts Council of Great Britain and the Association Française d'Action Artistique, The Hayward Gallery, London, January 24–April 5, 1970, no. 33. Marble version, Grappe, no. 239.

REPRODUCTIONS (in Rodin's lifetime)

Riotor, *Auguste Rodin, Statuaire*, frontispiece.

XII. Ames du Purgatoire
(Souls of Purgatory). 1893.

6-1/16 x 4⅝ in. (15.4 x 11.7 cm.) *State 1.*
6-1/16 x 3⅞ in. (15.4 x 9.9 cm.) *State 2.*

State One
68 Musée Rodin.
Before signed in the plate "Rodin" at lower left; some pen
and ink lines drawn over the drypoint, especially on the
face of center figure and hair of seated figure. Grappe
(p. 89) notes that the print was found among Rodin's papers
and is possibly unique.

State Two
69 Pasadena Art Museum, gift of Mr. and Mrs. Edward C.
Crossett.
Signed in the plate "Rodin" at lower left; some lines
scraped out, particularly along hip and shoulder of seated
figure; burr worn and lines of even tone with almost no
modeling; printed in green ink on Japan vellum, dark brown
ink on laid paper and brown ink on heavy China paper and
all three included as original prints in deluxe edition of
Geffroy, *La Vie artistique*, frontispiece. Deluxe edition numbered from 1 to 15, text printed on Japan vellum, and numbered 16 to 30 on heavy China paper. The ordinary edition
includes one original print of *Souls of Purgatory* printed in
dark brown ink on laid paper.
Colls: Bibliothèque Nationale (two impressions, one black
ink on China paper, one brown ink on laid paper); Boston
Museum of Fine Arts; British Museum; Frick Art Reference Library, New York (ordinary edition, print still in
text); Minneapolis Institute of Arts; National Gallery of
Art, Washington; Philadelphia Museum of Art Library
(deluxe edition no. 19, all three prints still in text); Stadtköln, Wallraf-Richartz Museum; Stanford University
Museum of Art; University of Glasgow.

In the delicate drypoint composition *Souls of Purgatory*
(Fig. 68) Rodin sketched three women with light, scarcely
modeled contours, their hair in loose wisps and their arms
enlacing each other's under the sparse foliage of a sketchily
indicated tree. The composition evidently pleased Rodin,
for not only does it appear in state 2 of the drypoint (Fig.
69) used for the frontispiece of the second book in *La Vie
artistique*, a series on art written by his friend and supporter
Gustave Geffroy, but it was also made into a wood engraving by Beltrand and Dété which was published in 1899 and
again in 1902 in works about Rodin's art.[1] A comparison
of details shows that both the drypoint and the drawing
used for the woodcut (Fig. 70) were copied very closely
from a drawing in the Musée Rodin (Fig. 71). For the drypoint, a tracing must have been turned over and outlined
on the plate, because the print does not reverse the original
composition.

Words written in the margins of the definitive drawing
for the drypoint, "*égalité / fraternité / limbes / liberté / trois
grâces / la guerre*" (equality / fraternity / limbo / liberty /
three graces / war), explain the multiple interpretations
that were given to the drypoint composition in titles and in
the Rodin literature during his lifetime. "Limbo," signify-
ing the souls awaiting entry into heaven, was taken from
Rodin's reading of Dante and was reflected in the title
"Ames du Purgatoire" used by Delteil in 1910. In 1900
Léon Riotor also indicated Dante's *Divine Comedy* as the
source for the drypoint, though he specified Canto II of the
"Purgatory," which does not seem to apply: "These three
women who are in despair under the tree of sin, and in their
strong and graceful nudity throb under a fever of tears, in
whose eyes, according to the expression of [Dante] l'Ali-
ghieri, express the desire to cry. These are also the figures
of the second canto of the *Divine Comedy*, the Purgatory."[2]
Riotor suggests that the tree in the composition is the tree of
Eve's original sin. In the context of souls in purgatory the
tree would symbolize a faultless sin, like the original sin, of
those who through an accident, such as not receiving the
last rites, must await salvation in Purgatory.

Rodin had also written "three graces" on the definitive
drawing for the drypoint, a common association with three
women standing with arms entwined. The artist's other
words, "liberty, fraternity and equality," inscribed as well
on a second drawing of three women (Fig. 72), were an
association as frequent in the nineteenth century for three
nude women with arms entwined as The Three Graces
were in classical antiquity.

1. Maillard, *Auguste Rodin, Statuaire*, wood engraving by Beltrand and
Dété, between 84 and 85. Marx, *Les Pointes Sèches de Rodin*, wood engraving reproduced by photogravure, 11.
2. Riotor, *Auguste Rodin, Statuaire*, 27–28.

68

Rodin

69

70 *Three Women*. 1885–1893. Pencil (?), white gouache. Location and dimensions unknown. Reproduced from *Burlington Magazine*, November 1918, 176.

71 *Three Women*. 1885–1893. Pen and brown ink, pencil. 7-9/16 x 5¼ in. (19.2 x 13.3 cm.). MR 1964.

72 *Three Standing Women Embracing*. 1885–1893. Pen and black ink, gray wash, white gouache. 4 x 2⅝ in. (10.2 x 6.7 cm.); mount 4-3/16 x 3⅝ in. (10.6 x 9.2 cm.). MR 2011.

REPRODUCTIONS (in Rodin's lifetime)
Delteil, no. 11.

70

71

72

XIII. Contribution Receipt of the Special American Hospital in Paris for Wounds of the Face and Jaw. 1916.

7 x 4½ in. (17.8 x 11.4 cm.)

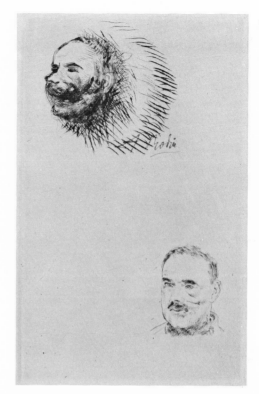

State One

73   Metropolitan Museum of Art, Whittelsey Fund, 1959 (cream wove paper).
Signed in pen "A Rodin."
Before signed in plate "Auguste Rodin 1916," composition without form letter.

State Two

74   The Fine Arts Museum of San Francisco.
Signed in plate "Auguste Rodin 1916," signature printed backward, composition with form letter; printed on thick textured wove paper as receipt for a contribution.
Colls: Bibliothèque Nationale; Metropolitan Museum of Art; Musée Rodin (five impressions); Philadelphia Museum of Art.

The year before his death Rodin made a drypoint showing a face disfigured from war wounds and the same head after surgery (Fig. 73). The composition was used to frame a printed receipt and expression of gratitude for contributions to a veteran's fund for war wounds of the face and jaw. State 2 of the drypoint (Fig. 74), includes the form letter receipt as well as the artist's signature "*Auguste Rodin 1916*," which appears backwards in the print. The form letter was written in English, in script at the center of the plate: "Dear / This is to acknowledge with deepest / thanks the receipt of your contribution of   to the fund for the / Special American Hospital in Paris / for wounds of the Face and Jaw / Respectfully Yours." Rodin had also helped the veteran's cause (possibly on the same occasion) by asking his friend Roger Marx, in an undated note, to exhibit a "small marble to profit the wounded veterans whose friends are organizing a small exhibition at 22, rue Caumartin."[1]

As a young man, Rodin had some exposure to the Franco-Prussian War in 1870–1871 when he served as a corporal in the 158th Regiment of the National Guard in Paris. The sculptor was undoubtedly sympathetic to the cause of reparation of facial disfigurement during World War I. He had devoted years of his life to understanding the relationship in portraiture between a man's physiognomy and his character and would have understood the implications of disfigurement for a young soldier.

In the upper face, Rodin projected the feeling of human anguish with the grimacing mouth, gaping slashed marks on the cheeks, and strange murky jaw. This sensation reverberates in the cross-hatched marks creating a barbed circle around the back of the skull and under the jaw and generating an open, confused silhouette. In contrast, the modeling of the lower head is softer, the profile and wounds closed and healed and the head comfortably set into the collar. Both heads appear to be those of a specific individual, which adds to the feeling of personal tragedy.

1. Undated letter from Rodin to Roger Marx. Roger Marx Collection of Letters, Sketches, and Notes of the Cathedrals of France, purchased from Claude Roger-Marx, Philadelphia Museum of Art, no. 21594.

Lithograph

75

L'Eternelle Idole
(The Eternal Idol). 1896–1905.
11 ⅛ x 8 ⅛ in. (28.4 x 20.6 cm.)

Unique State
75   Musée Rodin.
Coll: A second impression is in an unknown collection.

The only lithograph known to be by Rodin's hand[1] (Fig. 75) was drawn from the left three-quarters view of his plaster sculpture *The Eternal Idol* of 1889 (Fig. 76), with the lithograph reversing the image of the sculpture. In 1910 Delteil notes that there were two impressions of the lithograph, one retained by the artist and now in the Musée Rodin and one in Delteil's own collection. Delteil's impression was inscribed "*hommage à Monsieur Delteil A Rodin*" and later reproduced in the sales catalogue of Delteil's collection in 1928;[2] the lithograph was purchased by M. Caliac and the Galerie Caliac no longer has a record of the print.

Rodin was able to approach the medium of lithography, as he did drypoint, by drawing an image directly on a surface, in this case with the lithographic crayon on the stone. He worked with the grainy texture of the stone, building up layers of black, thinning out his strokes for gradations of tone and leaving a few strong highlights. The technique effectively translates the soft tonalities of his plaster sculpture *The Eternal Idol*. In a pencil drawing illustrating a marble or plaster sculpture for the *Gazette des Beaux-Arts* in 1905 (Fig. 77), Rodin created a comparable effect by using *estompe* or smudging his pencil strokes.

The lithograph appears unique and striking in Rodin's *œuvre* because the figures are so totally submerged in darkness, an experiment that probably owes its inception to the art of Eugene Carrière, as pointed out by Claude Roger-Marx:

Another incomparable lithograph is Rodin's *New Idol* which is later than his drypoints. His illustrations for the *Jardin des Supplices* were largely watercolours transferred to stone, but in *New Idol* two forms inter-penetrate each other, as do the light and shade. This unique plate, which shows the sculptor of *The Kiss* obtaining effects similar to those of Carrière's lithograph of Verlaine, is a testimony to the friendship that united these two artists.[3]

Degas, another artist during Rodin's period who showed the image coming out of complete darkness, worked in a "dark field manner" in some of his monotypes in which he covered the plate completely with ink and wiped the ink from those areas which formed the image. Edward Steichen's photographs of Rodin's sculpture from 1901 also partake in the aesthetic of using a dark background, like dusk to silhouette a sculpture such as *The Thinker* or *Balzac*, giving it only a few strong highlights. The lithograph *The Eternal Idol* may be distinguished from the work of Carrière and Steichen, though less from the monotypes of Degas, who was also a sculptor, in that Rodin's forms not only create the drama of luminosity but also the presence of a three-dimensional object.[4]

1. Grappe mentions that there were some early lithographs by Rodin done for a newspaper in Belgium in 1874; these have not been found at the Musée Rodin (Grappe, no. 251).
2. *Catalogue des Estampes Modernes Composant la Collection Loys Delteil*, 39.
3. Roger-Marx, *Graphic Art of the 19th Century*, 201.
4. A. Clot did some lithographic reproductions of Rodin's "black" drawings which are sometimes compared to *The Eternal Idol* and taken as original Rodin lithographs. A notable example is the lithograph after the *Horseman*, a drawing in the Art Institute of Chicago. The lithograph can be found in the collection of William Hayes Ackland Memorial Art Center, Chapel Hill, North Carolina, called *Figure on a Horse*; it was also published in Rainer Maria Rilke, *Auguste Rodin* (Leipzig: Insel-Verlag, 1922), no. 81, where it was given the ambiguous title "*Lithographie.*"

76

RELATED SCULPTURE
76 *The Eternal Idol.* 1889. Plaster. H. 29⅛ in. (74 cm.).
Musée Rodin.

RELATED DRAWING
77 *Figure of a Woman.* 1905. Pencil. Location and dimensions unknown. Reproduced from *Gazette des Beaux-Arts,*
June 1905.

REPRODUCTIONS (in Rodin's lifetime)
Delteil, no. 12.

77

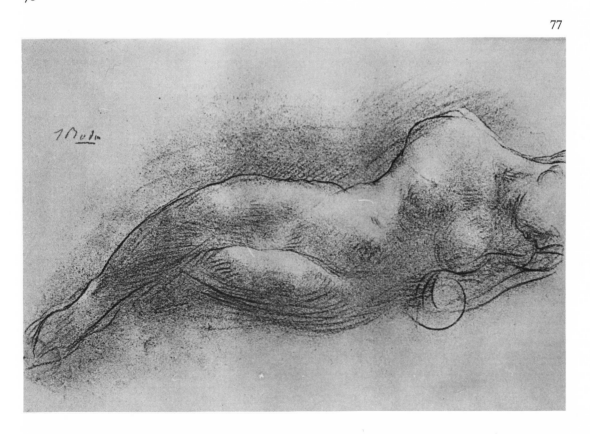

Book Illustrations

Introduction to Book Illustrations

The illustrations for *Le Jardin des Supplices* and *Les Elégies amoureuses d'Ovide* follow the oldest tradition of Western printed book illustration, originating in Europe in the 1460's, in which a professional engraver reproduces drawings of the master artist. For *Le Jardin des Supplices* of 1899, Auguste Clot made twenty-one lithographs after Rodin's drawings which were done so skillfully that it is difficult to discern the differences. For *Les Elégies amoureuses d'Ovide*, L. Perrichon cut woodblocks after the artist's drawings. The more recent practice of artists making original prints for books, the *livres de peintres* begun in the mid-nineteenth century, was developed under the sensitive care of the publisher Vollard from 1900 and continues with great popularity today. Rodin only once made an original print for a book, the drypoint *Souls in Purgatory* for the frontispiece of *La Vie artistique* in 1893.

The *livres de peintres* idea arose, after the advent of photography, in reaction to adoption by publishers of photomechanical reproduction of artist's drawings, a method less expensive and generally poorer in quality than the work of professional reproductive engravers. Like other artists of his period, Rodin complained about the quality of all types of photographic reproduction, preferring at times during the early 1880's to make his own drawings after his sculptures for catalogues (Figs. i and ii) rather than use mediocre photographs. As he became established, however, he complained as bitterly about his limited time and was prepared to accept high quality facsimile reproduction and good photographs. He was greatly pleased with Edward Steichen's artistic photographs of his sculptures from 1901 and even tried to persuade him to do the photography for the reproduction of a group of his drawings in an album to be published by the Insel-Verlag. Speaking of the drawings, Steichen related, "He [Rodin] has it in his head that I have to photograph them in order to reproduce them. . . ."[1]

It is understandable, then, that Rodin agreed to the high quality photographic reproduction of his two drawings illustrating Bergerat's *Enguerrande* in 1884. Rodin probably would have also approved of the excellent photographic facsimiles of his drawings for Baudelaire's *Les Fleurs du Mal*, published in 1918, the year after his death, in view of the fact that he had already accepted the facsimile album of his drawings done by the Maison Goupil in 1897 in which one Baudelaire illustration was reproduced using the same facsimile technique. He even exhibited this album on a table of his sculpture pavillion at the Exposition Universelle of 1900.

The Maison Goupil album as well as the prospective album of Rodin's drawings to be photographed by Steichen are in the same category as the albums and books in which numerous Rodin drawings were reproduced, and which must be distinguished from the four books he illustrated. The purpose of quality book illustration is to enhance the aesthetic value of a volume by juxtaposing visual and literary works in a meaningful relationship. To this end, Rodin collaborated with the author, publisher, or engraver, and sometimes with all three in illustrating four books. The records of his collaborations, which are discussed in this catalogue in connection with each book, have been reconstructed from the preparatory drawings, letters and contracts. In general, the documents show Rodin taking great pains to produce beautiful drawings appropriate to the text and receiving little commercial reward for his efforts. For the *Le Jardin des Supplices* he was to give up all rights to the drawings in exchange for two copies of the book, although the contract was later amended to give him four books, still a very small compensation.[2] His illustration of *Les Fleurs du Mal* with masterful drawings made directly along the margins of a text produced a volume in 1888 called "unique and priceless" two years later.[3] He complained to Edmond de Goncourt that he would have wished to spend more time, delving deeper into the meaning of the text, but was not adequately remunerated:

He spoke to me about the illustrations for Baudelaire's poetry, which he is in the midst of executing for an amateur and into the depths of which he would have liked to descend but the remuneration does not permit him to give it enough time. Thus, for this book which will not have publicity and which will stay closed in the cabinet of the amateur, he does not feel the zest, the fire of illustration, demanded by an editor.[4]

By contrast, a letter agreement (dated April 1904) between an editor of the *Gazette des Beaux-Arts* and Rodin for a proposed album of Rodin's drawings seems to indicate that their intent was "to spread his art" by exposing his drawings to a wider audience and for commercial gain as as well:

We are very glad M. Clot and myself to make these sacrifices [they bore the expense of the prospectus] to spread your art as much as it is in our power to do so, and we would be the first to rejoice in a success of which all the merit will be yours. But you will also understand, dear master, that we can start the work only if the subscription received through the prospectus is enough to cover the expenses of publication. It is understood that the profit resulting from the sale, after the expenses are deducted will be shared equally between you and the GBA.[5]

In addition to albums of his drawings reproduced by the lithographs of A. Clot, the colored etchings of H. Boutet, the wood engravings of L. Lepère, and the high quality photogravure of the Maison Goupil,[6] there are five books of poems in which Rodin's late drawings were reproduced.[7] Four of the books were published in London, and very little is known about Rodin's part in their production. One uses lithographs of Clot after Rodin's drawings and, not even claiming to be illustrated by Rodin, it is titled *Seven Lithographs by Clot from the Water-Colours of Auguste Rodin, with a chaplet of verse by Aleichester Crowley.* Among the records at the Musée Rodin showing drawings released and returned between 1898 and 1911, most of them with Clot's signature, only two have specific designations, one for M. Crowley (in Rodin's hand)[8] and the other for *Le Jardin des Supplices.* Without additional documentation, it is not possible to know whether Rodin took a greater part in the production of the five books of poems than he did in the albums reproducing his drawings.

1. Undated letter from Edward Steichen to Alfred Stieglitz, with an inscription "received late in 1913." The Alfred Stieglitz Archive, Collection of American Literature, Beinecke Rare Book and Manuscript Library, Yale University. The complete quotation of the passage follows: "Rodin is continually talking about another book of his drawings. He has it in his head that I have to photograph them in order to reproduce them and every time I try to explain he gets peevish and says I am simply trying to get out of it!! The Insel Verlag offered to do the work and he turned them over to me and I turned them down. . . ."

2. The contract is reproduced in the discussion of *Le Jardin des Supplices.*

3. Riotor, *Auguste Rodin, Statuaire,* 28: "*On cite un exemplaire des* Fleurs du Mal, *unique et sans prix, entièrement orné de sa main.*"

4. Goncourt, *Journal des Goncourt,* 227. *Jeudi, 29 décembre, 1887.*

5. Letter dated April 30, 1904, to Rodin from an editor (whose signature is illegible) at the *Gazette des Beaux-Arts,* 8, rue Favart, Paris. The long letter stipulates all of the details of publication including costs, number of copies, paper type, etc. It also states that Rodin will furnish the *GBA* with a list of amateurs with sufficient means and interest to buy the album. A copy of this list, dated May 10, 1905, is also in the Musée Rodin archives in the folder on A. Clot. I have not been able to find the album, and it was probably never sufficiently subscribed to cover the costs since the price was set at "100 copies sold at the high price 200F each. . . . 5 copies on Japan paper would be sold for 100F each."

6. See SELECTED BIBLIOGRAPHY, *Albums Reproducing Rodin Drawings During His Lifetime.*

7. See SELECTED BIBLIOGRAPHY, *Literary Works Reproducing Rodin Drawings During His Lifetime.*

8. Note in Rodin's handwriting, dated November 2, 1904. Musée Rodin archives, A. Clot folder. "*Remis à M. Crowley. 2 dessins (anglaise) / 1 petit dessin Jeune fille couchée sur un lit pour être, lithographe nouveaux, en feuille, sans numéro. / par M. Rodin le 2 novembre 1904 Meudon.*"

I. Emile Bergerat. «Enguerrande»

Paris: Bibliothèque des Deux-Mondes, Frinzine, Klein, et Cie., 1884. Preface by Théodore de Banville. Frontispiece portrait of Mirbeau by Henri Lefort. Two illustrations by Auguste Rodin. Page size: 11¼ x 9¼ in. (28.5 x 23.5 cm.). Illustrations commissioned 1884; first version of drawings completed by July 30, 1884. Book published October 25, 1884. The two illustrations are facsimile reproductions of Rodin's drawings.
Edition number unspecified.
Colls: Bibliothèque Nationale; Philadelphia Museum of Art Library.

In July 1884 Emile Bergerat wrote Rodin asking him to make changes in one of the two drawings illustrating his play *Enguerrande*. The play was published in October, and in November Bergerat wrote Rodin, "What a success! Your drawings are magnificent."[1] The rare and important letter of July 30, 1884, shows that Rodin illustrated specific scenes from the play and discussed the modification of both the subject and style of one of the illustrations, evidently at the request of the editor:

30 July 1884.

My dear friend,

Here are the proofs of your drawings. They came out well and you must be satisfied. But the editor writes to me here that the one that is standing up will get the bourgeois subscribers yapping. My feeling is that one must listen to that man.

Could you not, for the scene in the cabin sketch a woman (resumé of forms: twenty years old) in the style of Botticelli for example. It is not necessary to have a black background. It is a drawing of a sculptor not of a painter and the bearing and contour are what is of interest coming from your hand.

You would be very kind to do that immediately because we are proceeding firmly and quickly and one has to be ready. Perhaps you are less busy now than you used to be.

Here everybody is fine and as for me, I am swimming in laziness. Come and see us.

Warm greetings yours,
Emile Bergerat[2]

The letter refers to the first illustration (Fig. 78) placed in the text before Act II, where it illustrates scene 2 in which the queen Enguerrande enters a fisherman's cabin after being washed ashore in a storm at sea. The text says "the cabin is blackish" and the fisherman tells the queen to dry herself and dress below in the cabin "with all due respect, my queen, as if you would be a simple siren." Evidently this description suggested a dark background and a sensuous woman, and in the pen and ink drawing that was probably the first illustration submitted (Fig. 78a) Rodin drew a voluptuous nude in full front view with her arms coquettishly poised and her head to one side. After Bergerat's

request, Rodin changed the pose to a somewhat more demure profile view of a woman with long Botticelli-like hair, shielding her breasts with her arms (Fig. 78). The first version of the illustration was drawn from the live model standing in an academic pose with one foot on the model stand, but the second version is clearly after the statue *Eve* of 1881 (Fig. 78c) with the gesture of shame of the upper half of her body changed to an expression of modesty. In both compositions Rodin used the same chair and window at upper left. In the second, Rodin added a door at the right and lightened the background, which Bergerat had felt was too dark because it suggested a painter's atmospheric effect. Rodin's adaptation of his statue *Eve* also appears to respond to Bergerat's request that the bearing and contour of the figure clearly reflect the hand of the sculptor, whose reputation was just beginning to ascend.

A preparatory drawing for the final version of *Enguerrande in the Fisherman's Cabin* (Fig. 78b) shows Rodin's current practice in his drawings after sculpture of first outlining the contours and then filling in with hachure. While the preparatory drawing shows some crosshatching in the upper body, the final version has only parallel hachure, and it appears that Rodin made the decision to change his mode after working on the top half of the preparatory drawing. These alternative modes are characteristic of Rodin's drawings after sculpture, as seen in the web of crosshatching for the *John the Baptist* drawing (Fig. i) versus the fine, undulating parallel lines of the drawing after the J.-P. Laurens bust (Fig. ii).

The second illustration (Fig. 79), inserted in the text before the final Act V, shows Enguerrande and Gaëtan, the sculptor-prince, dead at the end of the play. The description calls for figures "stretched out dead, side by side and hands together, beneath a tent, at the approach to a battle field." Rodin chose to omit the tent and use the field as a backdrop. In the foreground he placed the foreshortened, gray, nude corpse of a man, reminiscent of representations of the dead Christ. Alongside him lies the white corpse of a woman whose body is copied from the back view of his sculpture *The Martyr* or from the same figure in the sculpture group *Paolo and Francesca* (Fig. 79a).

1. Letter from Emile Bergerat to Rodin, dated November 2, 1884. Musée Rodin archives, Bergerat folder. "*2 nov. 84 / Ami Rodin / Venez donc! . . . Quel succès! Vos dessins sont magnifiques! Votre ami / Emile Bergerat / 12 rue Vernier / Votre exemplaire est en reserve!*"
2. Letter from Emile Bergerat to Rodin, dated July 30, 1884. Musée Rodin archives, Bergerat folder. "*30 juillet 84 / à Saint Luroire Ile et Vilaine / Mon cher ami / Voici les épreuves de vos dessins. Ils sont bien venus et vous devrez*"

être satisfait. Mais l'éditeur m'écrit ici que celui debout va faire gueuler les bourgeois-souscripteurs. A mon sentiment il faut écouter cet homme. / Ne pourriez vous pour la scène de la cabane tracer une femme (resumé des formes: 20 ans dans le goût du Botticelli par exemple). Il est inutile d'y mettre un fond noir. C'est un dessin de statuaire non pas de peintre et l'allure et les contours sont ce qui interesse de votre main. / Vous seriez bien gentil de faire cela dès maintenant car nous marchons ferme et vite et il faut être prêt. Peut-être êtes vous moins occupé que vous l'étiez. / Tout le monde va bien ici et moi, je nage dans la paresse. Venez nous voir. / Mille amitiés de votre / Emile Bergerat."

78 *Enguerrande in the Fisherman's Cabin.* Act II, scene 2. Philadelphia Museum of Art Library.

78a *Enguerrande in the Fisherman's Cabin.* Pen and ink. Location and dimensions unknown. Reproduced from *Catalogue des tableaux modernes formant la collection de M. Jacques Zubaloff,* Galerie Georges Petit, Paris, June 16–17, 1927, no. 69.

78b Preparatory drawing for Fig. 78. Pen and ink, 12 x 7 in. (30.5 x 17.8 cm.). Martin Revson, private collection, New York City.

78c *Eve.* 1881. Plaster. H. 29-15/16 in. (76 cm.). The Fine Arts Museums of San Francisco.

79 *Enguerrande and Gaëtan Lying Dead.* Act V, scene 7. Philadelphia Museum of Art Library.

79a *Paolo and Francesca.* 1887. Plaster. H. 14 ⅛ in. (36 cm.). Musée Rodin. An earlier version for the *Gates of Hell* may have existed before 1884.

78

78a

78b

78c

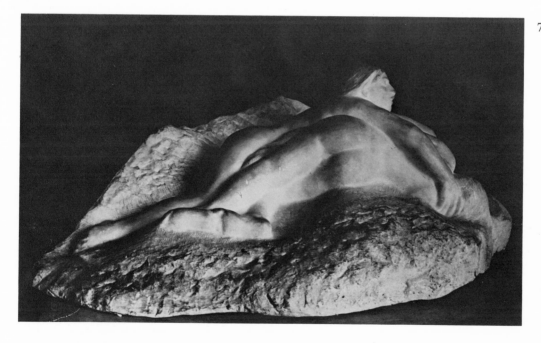

II. Charles Baudelaire. « Les Fleurs du Mal »

Paris: Poulet-Malassis et de Broise, 1857. Edition of book owned by Paul Gallimard illustrated with original drawings by Auguste Rodin; facsimile of dedication letter from Charles Baudelaire to Theophile Gautier; on half-title page, inscription in Baudelaire's handwriting: "à mon ami A. Lemaréchal. Ch. Baudelaire." Page size: 7⅜ x 4¾ in. (18.7 x 12 cm.).
Illustrations commissioned by Gallimard in 1887, completed in 1888. 27 pen and ink drawings made directly on Gallimard's book: 25 in margins and 5 inserted *hors texte* (4 of the 5 with watercolor added).
Coll: Musée Rodin (unique copy).

Charles Baudelaire. *Vingt-Sept Poèmes des Fleurs du Mal.*
Paris: La Société des "Amis du Livres Moderne," 1918.
Preface by Camille Mauclair. Illustrated by Auguste Rodin. Errata slip gives correct title, *Vingt-cinq poèmes de Baudelaire, illustrés de vingt-sept dessins de Rodin.* Page size: 7¼ x 4⅝ in. (18.4 x 11.7 cm.).
Illustrations are facsimiles of original drawings in Gallimard's book.
Edition of 200: 125 for members of the Society; 15 for collaborators; 60 for booksellers of the Society.
Colls: Bibliothèque Nationale; New York Public Library, Spencer Collection (copy no. 10); Philadelphia Museum of Art Library (copy no. 178).
References: Hofer, *The Artist and the Book, 1860–1960, in Western Europe and the United States,* 177.

Charles Baudelaire. *Les Fleurs du Mal.*
Paris: The Limited Editions Club, 1940. Preface by Camille Mauclair. Illustrated by Auguste Rodin. Book enlarged; more poems and wider margins. Page size: 9 x 7½ in. (23 x 19 cm.).
Illustrations are facsimiles of original drawings in Gallimard's book.
Edition of 1,500 numbered copies.
Colls: Bibliothèque Nationale; The Houghton Library, Department of Printing and Graphic Arts, Harvard University; Newberry Library, Chicago; New York Public Library, Rare Book Room (copy no. 898); University of Michigan, Ann Arbor; University of Virginia at Charlottesville.

Charles Baudelaire. *Vingt-cinq Poèmes des Fleurs du Mal.*
Paris: Les Peintres du Livre, 1968. Illustrated by Auguste Rodin.

Illustrations are facsimiles of original drawings in Gallimard's book; quality of facsimiles not as high as in 1918 and 1940 editions.
Edition of 3,000 numbered copies; 50 additional copies marked H. C. (*hors commerce*) for the publisher and collaborators.

80   Front cover of copy of *Les Fleurs du Mal* owned by Paul Gallimard. Musée Rodin.

81   *Embracing Lovers.* c. 1880–1888. Pencil, pen and ink, ink wash. 5⅝ x 3¾ in. (14.3 x 9.5 cm.). MR 5630. Reproduced as "Cercle des Amours" in *Les Dessins d'Auguste Rodin.*

In late December of 1887 Rodin told Edmond de Goncourt that he was in the midst of illustrating a copy of Baudelaire's *Les Fleurs du Mal* for a private collector.[1] In the following year Rodin signed the last of twenty-seven illustrations, "drawings commissioned of Rodin by M. Gallimard 1888." Five drawings were inserted in the book *hors texte* and twenty-two were made directly on Paul Gallimard's copy of an 1857 edition of *Les Fleurs du Mal* which was bound in brown leather with the design of a skull and thistle plant tooled on the front cover (Fig. 80). Rodin echoed the thistle motif in the crown or halo of the Devil in a drawing which he originally planned as the frontispiece[2] but later used as the second illustration (Fig. 83).

At the front of Gallimard's book is a letter to him from Rodin pasted in as a separate leaf. The letter lists eighteen[3] of the twenty-seven illustrated poems, the page number of the illustration, and Rodin's system of categorizing their style: "Those which are marked with an 'O' are line drawings (*au trait*), those with an 'X' are shaded (*ombrées*)." The letter continues, "I shall make 2 or 3 more line drawings and bring you the work." Among these drawings may have been the new frontispiece which was a line drawing added *hors texte* (Fig. 82) or some of the new line drawings transferred to the book by tracing. No evolution in style between the first eighteen drawings mentioned in the letter and those added later is discernible since both groups include refined examples of all of the modes used.

The pure line drawings relate to the drypoint *Figure Studies* (Fig. 5) while those with additional contours and light parallel lines of shading like *l'Aube Spirituelle* (Fig. 93) resemble the drypoint *La Ronde* (Fig. 18). Illustrations that Rodin considered "shaded" were those that used his

80

81

hachure technique, where the line fluctuates with minute body variations and imparts strong background shadows as in the drypoint *Henri Becque* (Fig. 25) and the illustrations for Bergerat's *Enguerrande* (Figs. 78 and 79).

Thematic sources for the *Les Fleurs du Mal* illustrations include both Rodin's interpretation of these poems at the time he did the illustrations in 1887–1888 and earlier inspiration by Baudelaire and Dante for the *Gates of Hell* sculptures commissioned in 1880.[4] Rainer Maria Rilke, the German poet who was Rodin's secretary in 1905, tells us that as a source of inspiration for the *Gates of Hell* "from Dante he (Rodin) came to Baudelaire."[5] Among the sculptures for the *Gates of Hell*, the tragic groups, *Ugolino* and *Paolo and Francesca* (Fig. 79a) derive from Dante's *Inferno*. Other tormented figures relate both to Dante's medieval vision of the inferno, where salvation was possible through a prescribed path of ascension, and to Baudelaire's nineteenth-century hell where man without Faith was cut off from salvation. From these two sources Rodin formulated his own vision of inferno for the *Gates of Hell*, as Judith Cladel explains: "Dante inspired this monstrous yet ennobled masterpiece, and Baudelaire's poetry filled many of its chinks and crannies with ignoble writhing shapes; shapes of dusky fire that, as they tumultuously stand above the gulf of fear, wave ineffectual and desperate hands as if imploring destiny."[6]

Rodin's drawing of embracing lovers (Fig. 81), showing sinners who might have existed in the hell of Dante or Baudelaire, provides evidence that Rodin drew inspiration from both poets. This is indicated by the inscriptions "Virgil/Dante" at the top of the drawing and "love profound as the grave / Baudelaire" at the bottom. The theme of death and suffering as a symbol of a late nineteenth-century malaise was also seen commonly in Salon sculptures which used subjects from Dante, particularly the theme of Ugolino. The more controversial and partially censored poems of Baudelaire appealed to fewer artists, among them Alphonse Legros, who illustrated the poems in 1861, and Odilon Redon, who illustrated them in 1890.

As an illustrator Rodin revealed his own interpretations of the poems in *Les Fleurs du Mal* through his manner of copying and adapting both his sculptures and drawings for the illustrations. In some poems he concentrated on the resonance between the poem's mood and his own symbol for the same emotion, such as the desperate mood of *Réversibilité* which he had symbolized in earlier sculpture and drawings as a seated man with his head cradled in his arms (Figs. 92a and 92b). More often, Rodin sought to physi-

cally embody both the poem's mood and Baudelaire's bizarre characters: his devils, his *femmes fatales*, a woman's nude corpse rotting or enshrined, a headless martyr, lovers intertwined.

1. Goncourt, *Journal des Goncourt*, 227. *Jeudi, 29 décembre, 1887.* See introduction to ILLUSTRATIONS section of this catalogue for a quotation of the complete passage.

2. See footnote 3 below for reasons why the drawing was probably first planned as the frontispiece.

3. The pages of the letter from Rodin to Gallimard list seventeen drawings for the illustrations of *Les Fleurs du Mal*. The eighteenth, noted on the back of the second sheet, is referred to as "Frontispiece—X." Since the "X" was Rodin's designation for a shaded drawing, the eighteenth drawing could not have been the pure line drawing ultimately used as the frontispiece but was probably the shaded drawing illustrating *Au Lecteur* which faced the dedication page.

4. For a discussion of the *Gates of Hell* including their relationship to the poetry of Dante and Baudelaire see Elsen, *Rodin's Gates of Hell.*

5. Rainer Maria Rilke, *Rodin*, trans. by Jessie Lemont and Hans Trausil, London: Grey Walls Press, 1946, 13.

6. Cladel, *Rodin the Man and His Art*, xii.

82   *L'Imprévu* (*The Unexpected*). 1887–1888. Pen and ink. 7⅜ x 4¾ in. (18.7 x 12 cm.). Musée Rodin. Frontispiece.*
82a   *Satan and Worshiper*. c. 1887–1888. Pencil, pen and ink, brown ink wash, white gouache. 4-7/16 x 5¾ in. (11.3 x 14.6 cm.). Inscribed above on mount "*à mon ami Will Rothenstein A. Rodin;*" below on drawing, "*serpent;*" below on mount, "Baudelaire." Collection Mr. and Mrs. A. Ward, Bakewell, England.

* For all subsequent illustrations, the caption will include the title of the poem, the medium and the page numbers in the 1857 edition, the 1918 edition and the 1940 edition, respectively. Date, dimensions and collection remain the same throughout. Related works will be numbered as Fig. 82a, etc.

With the first drawing, the frontispiece illustrating *L'Imprévu* (Fig. 82), Rodin immediately plunges the reader into the depths of hell by showing him a naked youth worshipping Satan by committing the cardinal sin of an anal embrace. At the bottom of the drawing Rodin wrote a passage from *L'Imprévu*, a poem which was not included in *Les Fleurs du Mal*:

> You have in secret, kissed my filthy ass.
> Know Satan by his conquering laugh,
> As outrageous and ugly as the world!
> (*Vous avez, en secret, baisé ma fesse immonde.*
> *Reconnaissez Satan à son rire vainqueur,*
> *Enorme et laid comme le monde!*)

The fine contour drawing for *L'Imprévu* was traced from a heavily layered, ink and gouache drawing of the same subject inscribed "*serpent*" (Fig. 82a) and "Baudelaire." The drawing was inspired by the Black Mass of the witches' Sabbath where the ritual of Satan worship included an anal embrace. When the subject was traced for the illustration of *L'Imprévu*, Rodin made the iconography more obvious by giving the devil pointed ears and claws on his hands and feet, and by adding large, puckered lips to the youth who kisses Satan's bottom.

83   *Au Lecteur* (*To the Reader*). Pen and ink. Opposite dedication page; 10; xiv.
83a   *Walking Male Nude*. c. 1875–1880. Pen and ink. Location and dimensions unknown. Reproduced from *Revue Populaire des Beaux-Arts*, special issue devoted to Rodin, April 8, 1899, 212.

Like the drawing for *L'Imprévu*, the drawing for the poem *Au Lecteur* (Fig. 83) was first traced from an earlier sketch of a nude male figure (Fig. 83a), then pointed demonic ears were added to the head. The left hand with its claw-like fingers is similar in both drawings. Behind the head of the standing nude in *Au Lecteur*, Rodin added a spiked leaf motif, similar to the thistle leaves on the leather book cover, which appears as a crown or halo to the demonic figure. As the demon looks back over his shoulder, he beckons or reaches out with his right hand in a gesture similar to that of Virgil as he guides Dante through hell in two of Rodin's drawings (Fig. 103a).[1] With the spiked crown, the pointed ears, one claw hand and one beckoning hand, the figure embodies Baudelaire's guide, the Devil in the passage of *Au Lecteur*:

> The Devil jerks the strings, O subtle guide!
> All round us loathsome objects cast their spell;
> Each day we sink a little nearer Hell
> And pass through foetid glooms, unhorrified.[2]

1. The second drawing of Dante and Virgil is reproduced in Elsen, *Rodin's Gates of Hell*, pl. 15.
2. The following translation has been used throughout: *Flowers of Evil* (*Les Fleurs du Mal*), *Poems of Baudelaire*, rendered into English by Florence Louie Friedman, introduction by Richard Church, London: Elek Books, 1962.

84   *Bénédiction* (*The Blessing*). Pen and ink. 14; 18; 6.
84a   *Orpheus and Eurydice*. c. 1893. Marble. H. 50 in. (127 cm.). The Metropolitan Museum of Art, gift of Thomas F. Ryan, 1910.

83

83a

84

84a

85

85a

For the illustration of the poem *Bénédiction* (Fig. 84) Rodin closely copied his sculpture group *Orpheus and Eurydice* (Fig. 84a), which was carved in marble by his workshop in 1893 but must have existed in a clay or plaster version in 1888. The only changes from the sculpture are that Eurydice is crowned with leaves and her nude legs which touch the ground in the marble are draped and float off to the side in the illustration. Orpheus' hand, in the sculpture, hides his eyes to avoid looking at Eurydice, while in the illustration Rodin moved Orpheus' hand down to his cheek and turned the palm out to create the gesture of shame from his statue *Eve* (Fig. 78c). Eurydice, now crowned (perhaps with a poet's wreath of laurels) and floating in air, represents a guardian angel; and Orpheus, with a gesture of shame or rejection, becomes the outcast poet of Baudelaire's passage:

> Yet, guarded by an Angel's secret care,
> The sun intoxicates this outcast child.

85   *Le Guignon* (*Ill Luck*). Pen and ink. 35; 20; 18.
85a   *Toilet of Venus.* c. 1886. Bronze. H. 18 1/8 in. (46 cm.). Musée Rodin. (Derives from *Kneeling Fauness,* c. 1884, plaster, left side of tympanum of *Gates of Hell*; reproduced in Grappe, no. 109.)

In the poem *Le Guignon*, Baudelaire used a metaphor to describe the poet's struggle to create:

> Many a flower reluctantly
> Spills its fragrance secretly
> In deep and hidden solitudes.

To Rodin the metaphor suggested the image of a resistive temptress, the *femme fatale* of the nineteenth century. For the illustration (Fig. 85) he copies his sculpture *Toilet of Venus* (Fig. 85a), her arms raised in a gesture of seduction, her nude, curvacious torso frontal, her face and eyes averted, and her flowing hair lengthened.

86   *La Beauté* (*Beauty*). Pen and ink. 47; 22; 26.

Rodin's illustration for *La Beauté* (Fig. 86), the nude torso of a woman with her head turned to one side, is based on his sculpture *Meditation*. In the poem *La Beauté*, Baudelaire knits together several features of the nineteenth-century *femme fatale*: her hard "breast where all are bruised in turn," her supreme position as "throned, a mysterious sphinx," her lack of compassion ("never do I laugh and never weep"), and her eyes as cold unseeing mirrors. Baudelaire's embellishments of the archetypal *femme fatale* may have encouraged Rodin's own variations on this theme in the illustra-

tions for both *La Beauté* and *Le Guignon* as well as in numerous sculptures of the subject.

Meditation. c. 1885. Bronze. H. 57 in. (145 cm.). Figure on the right side of the tympanum of *Gates of Hell*. Reproduced in Grappe, no. 127. The figure was also the model for a muse in the *Monument to Victor Hugo*, and separate statues of it were sometimes given titles derived from that context, such as *The Muse* and *The Inner Voice*, the latter from Hugo's poems *Les Voix Intèrieures*.

87   *Les Bijoux* (*Jewels*). Pen and ink. 53; 24; 258.

For *Les Bijoux* (Fig. 87) Rodin drew the figure of his sculpture *The Thinker* and surrounded it with heavy hachure so that the seated male nude would appear more solidly rooted to the rock where he sits. In the illustration for *Les Bijoux*, the figure of *The Thinker* symbolizes the poet's isolated soul grounded to a "crystal rock." From this vantage point the poet's soul is tempted by the seductive beckoning of his mistress just as *The Thinker*, the solitary nexus for the *Gates of Hell*, observes the multiple manifestations of desire and sin taking place beneath him.

The Thinker. 1888. Bronze. H. 27 1/8 in. (69 cm.). Plaster model before 1888. Figure at the center of *Gates of Hell*. Reproduced in Grappe, nos. 55–56.

88   *Une Charogne* (*A Carrion*). Pen and ink. 49, next to poem *L'Ideal*, but designated by Rodin for *Une Charogne*, 66; 28; 44.
88a   *Dying Woman and Skeleton.* c. 1885–1888. Pencil (contour lines and scribbled transfer lines on back of sheet), pen and brown ink (reinforced lines). 3 7/8 x 6-1/16 in. (9.8 x 15.4 cm.). Inscribed "*elle était de le monde où les plus belles choses ont le pire destin.*" MR 2037.
88b   *Dying Woman Attacked by Skeletons.* c. 1880–1888. Pencil, pen and ink, white gouache. 3 1/2 x 5-9/16 in. (8.9 x 14.1 cm.). Inscribed "*résurrection.*" MR 3776.

Rodin drew a nude woman lying on her side with her legs apart on page 49 next to the poem *L'Ideal* but later inscribed the drawing "page 66" to designate its new placement next to the poem *Une Charogne* (Fig. 88). The poet in *Une Charogne* explicitly describes a woman's rotting corpse and tells his mistress that she will soon resemble it. Rodin's illustration

Les poëtes devant mes grandes attitudes,
Qu'on dirait que j'emprunte aux plus fiers monuments,
Consumeront leurs jours en d'austères études;

Car j'ai pour fasciner ces dociles amants
De purs miroirs qui font les étoiles plus belles :
Mes yeux, mes larges yeux aux clartés éternelles !

86

Elle était donc couchée, et se laissait aimer,
Et du haut du divan elle souriait d'aise
A mon amour profond et doux comme la mer
Qui vers elle montait comme vers sa falaise.

Les yeux fixés sur moi, comme un tigre dompté,
D'un air vague et rêveur elle essayait des poses,
Et la candeur unie à la lubricité
Donnait un charme neuf à ses métamorphoses.

Et son bras et sa jambe, et sa cuisse et ses reins,
Polis comme de l'huile, onduleux comme un cygne,
Passaient devant mes yeux clairvoyants et sereins;
Et son ventre et ses seins, ces grappes de ma vigne,

S'avançaient plus câlins que les anges du mal,
Pour troubler le repos où mon âme était mise,
Et pour la déranger du rocher de cristal,
Où calme et solitaire elle s'était assise.

Je croyais voir unis par un nouveau dessin
Les hanches de l'Antiope au buste d'un imberbe,
Tant sa taille faisait ressortir son bassin.
Sur ce teint fauve et brun le fard était superbe !

— Et la lampe s'étant résignée à mourir,
Comme le foyer seul illuminait la chambre,
Chaque fois qu'il poussait un flamboyant soupir,
Il inondait de sang cette peau couleur d'ambre !

87

Ce qu'il faut à ce cœur profond comme un abîme,
C'est vous, Lady Macbeth, âme puissante au crime,
Rêve d'Eschyle éclos au climat des autans;

Ou bien toi, grande Nuit, fille de Michel-Ange,
Qui tors paisiblement dans une pose étrange
Tes appas façonnés aux bouches des Titans !

88

89

89a

of a nude corpse with her legs apart more appropriately fits the images of this poem than *L'Ideal* in which the poet compares dissipated female beauties to his more robust mistress.

The illustration was drawn either from the female figure in Rodin's sculpture group *Avarice and Luxury* or from an identical figure of a woman embraced by a skeleton of death in the drawing *Dying Woman and Skeleton* (Fig. 88a); the drawing is tellingly inscribed "she was of the world where the most beautiful things have the worst destinies." In another drawing (Fig. 88b) a nude woman lying on her back is voraciously kissed on the mouth by the skeleton of death while a second beauty, already decomposing, swoons backwards with her arms locked around the hips of the dying woman. These two drawings on the theme of death and the maiden indicate that although Rodin simplified his presentation for the illustration *Une Charogne* to omit the figure of death, his consideration of the theme in other drawings matched the gruesome power of Baudelaire's poem.

RELATED SCULPTURE NOT REPRODUCED
Avarice and Luxury. Before 1887. Plaster. H. 9 7/8 in. (25 cm.). Figure above the right tomb on *Gates of Hell.* Reproduced in Grappe, no. 175.

89 *De Profundis Clamavi* ("*Out of the depths, have I cried*"). Pen and ink, watercolor, gouache. Between 68 and 69 *hors texte*; opp. 28; opp. 44.
89a *Lovers Embracing.* c. 1880–1888. Pen and ink, black and brown ink wash, white gouache. 8-3/16 x 4-5/16 in. (20.8 x 11 cm.). MR 1947.

The full page ink and gouache drawing of a man reaching up in a vain attempt to embrace a woman (Fig. 89) illustrates the following lines of Baudelaire's poem, which Rodin wrote on the bottom of his drawing for *De Profundis Clamavi*:

> I implore your pity, You, the only one
> I love, from the depths of this dark abyss
> where my heart is fallen.
> (*J'implore ta pieté, Toi, l'unique que j'aime,*
> *Du fond du gouffre obscur où mon cœur est tombé.*)

The pose of the male figure was derived from Rodin's sculpture *Je Suis Belle*, the base of which was also inscribed with a Baudelaire poem about the unattainable *femme fatale*. The subject was repeated in several drawings (Fig. 89a), all virtually the same as the *De Profundis Clamavi* illustration except for one where the woman's legs are tucked under her to combine the pose of the Baudelaire illustration and the sculpture *Je Suis Belle*.

RELATED DRAWINGS NOT REPRODUCED
Couple with Woman's Leg Bent Under Her. c. 1880–1888.
Purple-blue ink (reproductive technique with reinforced
lines drawn on top). 7-11/16 x 4⅝ in. (19.5 x 11.5 cm.).
Inscribed ". . . *Hugo*." MR 376.
Couple. c. 1880–1888. Pen and ink, ink wash. 3-15/16 x
3-1/16 in. (10 x 7.8 cm.). MR 1913.
Couple. 1880–1888. Pen and ink, ink wash, white gouache.
8¼ x 5¼ in. (21 x 13.3 cm.). Inscribed "*poète . . . Baude . . .*"
MR 7109.
Couple. 1880–1888. Pen and ink, ink wash. Inscribed
"*l'étoile.*" Location and dimensions unknown. Reproduced
in *L'Art et les Artistes*, 1914, 76 (special issue devoted to
Rodin); and in *Les Dessins d'Auguste Rodin*, pl. 78.

RELATED SCULPTURE NOT REPRODUCED
Je Suis Belle. 1882. Plaster. H. 29½ in. (75 cm.). Reproduced
in Grappe, no. 85. Bronze version inscribed with first stanza
of poem from *Les Fleurs du Mal*, beginning, "*Je suis belle,
ô mortels! comme un rêve de pierre. . . .*"

90 *Remord Posthume* (*Remorse After Death*). Pen and ink.
78; 33; 49.

The nude figure illustrating *Remord Posthume* (Fig. 90)
derives from Rodin's sculpture *Toilet of Venus* (Fig. 85a), a
work which was also the model for the nude in the illustration for *Le Guignon* (Fig. 85). For *Remord Posthume*, however, the figure lies on her back amidst a delicately webbed
encasement which represents a grave. Rodin's image corresponds to the poem's first stanza:

> When you shall sleep forever, lovely shade,
> Within your marble tomb and winding sheet,
> Your only dwelling-place, your sole retreat,
> The damp and hollow grave where you are laid; . . .

91 *Tout Entière* (*Entirety*). Pen and ink. 85; 34; 61.

As in the illustration for the frontispiece and *Au Lecteur*,
Rodin chose to represent the Devil in his illustration for
Tout Entière (Fig. 91). He gave the image of the Devil wings
and a gliding gait in *Tout Entière*. With his back arched and
one leg lifted up, the figure evokes the poem's opening
lines:

> The Devil to my attic came
> Early this day to visit me,
> And seeking slyly cause for blame —
> "I want so much to know"—said he, . . .

RELATED DRAWINGS NOT REPRODUCED
Winged Figure. c. 1854–1864. Pen and ink. 3½ x 2⅛ in.
(8.9 x 5.4 cm.). MR 373. Although the exact prototype for
the illustration for *Tout Entière* is not known, this drawing

90

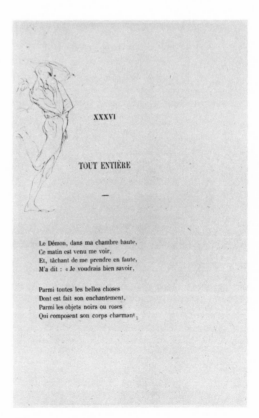

91

is among those of winged figures which may have served as examples; another is MR 5931, and a third is *Tomb Monument*, c. 1860–1875, pencil, 2 1/8 x 3 1/8 in. (5.4 x 7.9 cm.). inscribed "*un ange viendra allumer les flambeaux . . . ,*" Musée des Beaux-Arts de Lyon, gift of M. Fennaille, 1913.

92 *Réversibilité* (*Reversibility*). Pen and ink. 94; 36; 65.
92a *Man with Head in Arms.* 1887–1888. Pencil on thin tracing paper. 4 1/2 x 2 1/2 in. (11.4 x 6.4 cm.). Inscribed "*tombes.*" MR 5613. Reproduced in *Les Dessins d'Auguste Rodin*, pl. 8.
92b *Two Figures in Despair.* c. 1875–1885. Pencil, pen and ink, ink wash, white gouache. 4 1/2 x 3 1/4 in. (11.4 x 8.3 cm.). Inscribed "*icare Phaëton.*" MR 3759. Reproduced in *Les Dessins d'Auguste Rodin*, pl. 86.

The seated male nude with his head cradled in his arms in the illustration for *Réversibilité* (Fig. 92) was a symbol for despair that Rodin used in several drawings (Figs. 92a and 92b). The mournful attitude of these figures is echoed by one inscription "*tombes,*" written on the definitive drawing for the illustration (Fig. 92a). The poet's cries of sorrow struck a resonant note for Rodin:

> Angel of gladness, do you know despair,
> Shame and remorse and weariness and tears,
> Those nights of terror filled with tenuous fears, . . .

92

XL

RÉVERSIBILITÉ

—

Ange plein de gaîté, connaissez-vous l'angoisse,
La honte, les remords, les sanglots, les ennuis,
Et les vagues terreurs de ces affreuses nuits
Qui compriment le cœur comme un papier qu'on froisse?
Ange plein de gaîté, connaissez-vous l'angoisse?

Ange plein de bonté, connaissez-vous la haine,
Les poings crispés dans l'ombre et les larmes de fiel,
Quand la Vengeance bat son infernal rappel,
Et de nos facultés se fait le capitaine?
Ange plein de bonté, connaissez-vous la haine?

92a

92b

Man Seated on Rock with Leg Up. c. 1880–1888. MR 5583. Reproduced in Grappe, no. 46.

Man Seated with Head in Arms. c. 1864–1870. Pencil on lined notebook paper. 3¼ x 2⅜ in. (8.3 x 6 cm.). MR 389.

93 *L'Aube Spirituelle* (*The Spiritual Dawn*). Pen and ink. 100; 39; 69.
93a *Group of Figures.* c. 1870–1880. Pen and ink, white gouache. 4¼ x 5¾ in. (10.8 x 14.6 cm.). Inscribed "*les contemplations / les chats (?) / Hugo.*" MR 3757.
93b *Groups of Male Figures.* c. 1865–1875. Pen and ink. 7⅞ x 12⅛ in. (19.9 x 30.9 cm.). MR 2854.

The poem *L'Aube Spirituelle*, speaks of a spirit that awakes at the dawn within those debauched the night before: "An Angel in their brutish stupor wakes." Rodin's corresponding image (Fig. 93) is a tightly packed throng of nude male figures bent around a table; one of them stands in the middle, his arms flung out perhaps to symbolize an angel stirring his spirit. Several drawings of despondent male groups (Figs. 93a and 93b) consoling one another or grouped around a table, some taken from sarcophagi,[1] may have served as models to which Rodin then added the central gesturing figure.

1. Additional group compositions are reproduced and discussed in K. Varnedoe, "Early Drawings by Auguste Rodin," *Burlington Magazine*, April 1974, 197–202.

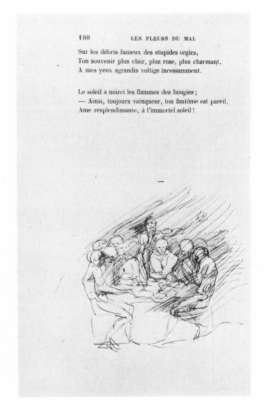

93

93a

93b

106   LES FLEURS DU MAL

Tout cela ne vaut pas le poison qui découle
De tes yeux, de tes yeux verts,
Lacs où mon âme tremble et se voit à l'envers ;
— Mes songes viennent en foule
Pour se désaltérer à ces gouffres amers.

Tout cela ne vaut pas le terrible prodige
De ta salive qui mord,
Qui plonge dans l'oubli mon âme sans remord,
Et , charriant le vertige,
La roule défaillante aux rives de la mort !

94

94   *Le Poison (Poison)*. Pen and ink. 106; 41; 73.
94a   *The Death of Adonis*. Before 1893. Marble. H. 14½ in. (36.8 cm.). Walters Art Gallery, Baltimore. Bronze version dates before 1888 (reproduced in Grappe, no. 226).

For the poem *Le Poison* Rodin copied his sculpture *The Death of Adonis* (Fig. 94a) in which the nude figure of Venus bends over the body of her dead lover. In the context of Baudelaire's poem, the tragic classical group (Fig. 94) takes on the contemporary connotation of man's ultimate destruction through woman's sexual love:

> All this is less than poisons cruelly strong
> Which, from your green eyes, seep;
> All this is less than your saliva's gall,
> That fearful prodigy
> Which steeps my soul in trance relentlessly,
> Till, dizzy in its thrall,
> Approaching Death, it swoons in ecstasy!

94a

By placing the embracing couple in the hollow vortex of a huge tree, Rodin's illustration emotes the poem's hallucinatory ecstasy of sex.

95   *L'Irréparable* (*The Irreparable*). Pen and ink, ink wash, white gouache. Between 118 and 119 *hors texte*; opp. 43; opp. 80.

Remorse eats away at the soul in Baudelaire's poem *L'Irréparable*:

> Can we suppress the old, the long Remorse,
> Writhing and stirring tirelessly,
> Eating us like the worm the dead, its course
> The caterpillar's in the tree?

To illustrate the poem, Rodin's symbol for a soul writhing in torment of remorse is a standing man with a snake coiled around his arm and stomach (Fig. 95). Ominous black shadows irradiated with flashes of white gouache add to the feeling of torment and suffocation.

RELATED DRAWINGS NOT REPRODUCED
Although the exact prototype for the illustration *L'Irréparable* has not been found, there are numerous drawings of figures with snakes as well as those inscribed "*serpent.*" Two of these drawings where the snake is clearly wrapped around a man's body follow:

Kneeling Man with Snake around His Neck. c. 1865–1875. Pencil, pen and ink. 2-13/16 x 2-11/16 in. (7.2 x 6.8 cm.). MR 407.

Man with Serpent around Torso and Legs. c. 1875–1889. Pen and ink, ink wash and watercolor. 6 x 4⅜ in. (15.2 x 11.1 cm.). Location and dimensions unknown. Reproduced in *Burlington Magazine*, November 1918, 177. Sold in Morin Sale at De Vries, Amsterdam, May 10–11, 1927.

96   *Causerie* (*Colloquy*). Pen and ink. 122; 48; 84.
96a *Couple Embracing Under the Moon.* c. 1875–1885. Pen and ink, gray wash, white gouache. 6-5/16 x 3¾ in. (16 x 9.5 cm.). Inscribed "*la nuit.*" MR 5623.
96b *Group of Despondent Figures.* c. 1875–1885. Pen, purple and black ink. 6¼ x 4-1/16 in. (15.9 x 10.3 cm.). Inscription mostly illegible: "*la groupe . . . figure . . . ememes . . . estampes. . . .*" MR 1930.

95

96

96a

96b

An embracing couple copied from one drawing (Fig. 96a) was combined with a group of despondent figures related to the composition of a second drawing (Fig. 96b) in what may be an allusion to two ideas from the poem *Causerie*. In the illustration (Fig. 96), the standing figure on the left, with his hair more disheveled and expression more agitated than in the preparatory drawing, holds to his breast a downcast partner (of undetermined sex); the couple may illustrate the passage "Gently your hand explores my ravished breast. You search beloved, a desecrated shrine."

On the other hand if both standing figures are men their embrace may be interpreted as a consoling gesture. They may symbolize, along with the three despondent foreground figures, shattered souls devastated by woman's sexual power. The poet in *Causerie* describes his ravaged heart:

> Women, with tooth and claw, have doomed your quest,—
> You seek a heart! Wild beast have gorged on mine. . . .
> O Beauty, scourge of souls, you crave your share!
> Then let your eyes, flaming like torch-lit feasts,
> Consume these shreds neglected by the beasts.

97

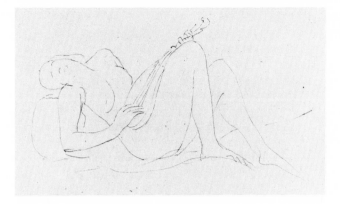

98

98a

97 *L'Irrémédiable* (*The Irremediable*). Pen and ink, water-color, gouache. Inscribed "*une ange imprudent voyager.*" Between 148 and 149 *hors texte*; 50; 152.

Rodin inscribed the words from the poem *L'Irrémédiable* "an angel imprudent traveler" on the ink and gouache draw-ing of a standing man with his legs desultorily crossed and his head couched dejectedly in his arms (Fig. 97), and the artist inserted the full-page drawing in the book to illustrate the poem. The knotted, agonized figure, surrounded by an oppressive black gloom, created out of layers of ink wash, gives substance to the lines:

> Trapped in a nightmare's huge distress,
> And, like a swimmer, spent and struggling,
> Fighting an agonizing doom
> Within a whirlpool vast and black, . . .

RELATED SCULPTURE NOT REPRODUCED
The Three Shades. 1880. Plaster. H. 75⅝ in. (192 cm.). Musée Rodin. Reproduced in Grappe, no. 59. Figures on the top center of *Gates of Hell.*

98 *Tristesse de la Lune* (*Sorrow of the Moon*). Pen and ink. 173; 55; 100.
98a *Woman Playing the Mandolin.* 1887–1888. Pencil, pen and ink. 2⅞ x 3-15/16 in. (7.3 x 10 cm.); mounted with fifteen other drawings on large sheet 10⅜ x 13¼ in. (26.4 x 33.7 cm.). MR 162.

99

The drawing of a woman holding a mandolin with a tiny quarter moon behind her (Fig. 98a) is an unusual subject in Rodin's *œuvre* and may have been created expressly to illustrate the poem *Tristesse de la Lune*. The moon, the cushion headrest, and the description of a woman's self caress, which Rodin represented by the metaphor of a woman playing the mandolin, all illustrate the poem's lines:

> Tonight the moon is musing languidly,
> And on her cushions like a beauty rests,
> Caressing with her hand abstractedly,
> Before she sleeps, the contours of her breasts.

In the final, traced illustration only the moon is omitted as the artist concentrated on a suave and more fluid body silhouette (Fig. 98).

99 *La Destruction* (*The Destruction*). Pen and ink. 182; 57; 214.
99a *Two Men Locked in Combat*. c. 1870–1888. Pencil. Brown ink strokes and ink inscription added in 1887–1888. 5-5/16 x 3¾ in. (13.5 x 9.5 cm.). Inscribed "*on s'y tue.*" MR 1946.

The exhausted sinner broken from the Devil's relentless seductions is shown one last vision in the poem *La Destruction*:

> He thrusts before my eyes, filled with confusion,
> Foul rags and open wounds till I, aghast,
> See all the blood-stained trappings of Destruction!

To illustrate this gruesome daydream, Rodin copied a pencil drawing of two "flayed" male figures locking each other in wrestler's holds (Fig. 99a). Probably in response to the meaning of the poem, Rodin added four pen lines extending from the back of the neck of the lower man toward the mouth of the one above in order to represent bitten flesh of an open wound. The grim spirit of the poem may also have inspired Rodin's pen notation at the top of the drawing, "*on s'y tue*" ("one gets killed there.") This mood is intensified in the final illustration where Rodin enlarged the area of the wound, made the figures' eyes bulge, and distended those muscles exerting the greatest strain (Fig. 99).

100 *Une Martyre* (*A Martyr*). Pen and ink. 183; 58; 215.

In the poem *Une Martyre* a painting of a martyr hangs in a room oppressively cluttered with art objects. To illustrate the headless martyr ("A headless corpse is letting forth a stream of blood"), Rodin drew his statue of a reclining

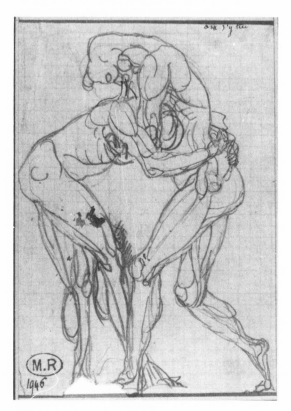

99a

woman with one leg bent under her, severed her head, showed blood spurting from her neck and placed the corpse dramatically above the poem's title (Fig. 100).

RELATED SCULPTURE NOT REPRODUCED
The Fatigue. 1887. Bronze. H. 6⅝ in. (17 cm.). Musée Rodin. Reproduced in Grappe, no. 179.

101   *Femmes Damnées* (*Women Accursed*). Pen and ink. 191; 62; 267.
101a   *Two Nude Women Embracing.* 1887–1888. Pen and brown ink. 3¾ x 5-9/16 in. (9.5 x 14.1 cm.). Inscribed "*le printemps. . . .*" MR 2013.
101b   *The Metamorphosis of Ovid.* Before 1886. Bronze. H. 7⅞ in. (20 cm.). Musée Rodin. The drawing *Two Nude Women Embracing* was copied from the more upright plaster version (reproduced in Grappe, no. 151).

Lesbian love, the subject of the poem *Femmes Damnées*, was candidly illustrated in Rodin's composition of two nude women entwined (Fig. 101). The illustration was traced from a delicate, pen and ink drawing of same size (Fig. 101a) which may have been executed expressly for the illustration. The drawing, in turn, was copied from Rodin's sculpture of the same composition variously titled *Metamorphosis of Ovid, Volupté,* and *Les Fleurs du Mal* (Fig. 101b). In both the sculpture and preparatory drawing, the more passive of the two women shields her face while the palm of one hand is turned outward in Eve's symbolic gesture of shame. In the *Femmes Damnées* illustration, however, the gesture of shame is omitted, the gap between the figures is closed, and the tense encounter of the earlier works has given way to a languid acquiesence more in consonance with Baudelaire's poem.

102   *Les Deux Bonnes Sœurs* (*The Two Good Sisters*). Pen and ink. 199; 68; 220.
102a   *Death and the Maiden.* 1880–1888. Pencil. Pen and ink lines added in 1887–1888. 5⅜ x 3⅜ in. (13.7 x 8.6 cm.). MR 1986.

A nude woman is coupled with the skeleton of death (Fig. 102) in a spirited dance to illustrate the first stanza of *Les Deux Bonnes Sœurs*:

> Debauchery and Death, two sisters kind
> And vigorous, with grim embraces free,
> Whose virgin wombs unsightly tatters bind,
> Are barren though in labour ceaselessly.

100

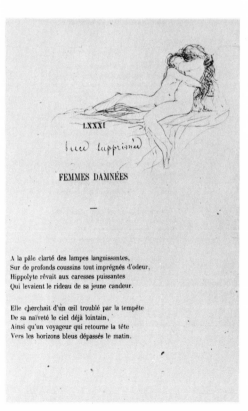

101a

101b

A pencil drawing of the dance of death (Fig. 102a), with several pen guide lines along the maiden's silhouette, was traced and elegantly simplified for the illustration. The pen strokes in the preparatory drawing which enlarge the maiden's abdomen represent Baudelaire's idea of the two women "in labour ceaselessly." Other pen strokes show Rodin's attempt to work out Death's gesture, which in the final illustration becomes a flaunting wave matching the hideous grin added to her face.

103   *La Béatrice (Beatrice)*. Pen and ink. 204; 69; 223.
103a   *Virgil Leading Dante*. c. 1880. Pen and ink, sepia and gouache. 6¾ x 4 in. (17.1 x 10.2 cm.). Inscribed "*Dante et Virgile effrayés par les démons qui surplombent à la descente du cercle*." MR 3768.

104   *La Béatrice (Beatrice)*, second illustration. Pen and ink, watercolor. Signed "Rodin." Between 204 and 205 *hors texte*; opp. 60; opp. 222.
104a   *A Woman and Three Men Dancing*. c. 1875–1885. Pen and ink, watercolor. Location and dimensions unknown. Formerly in collection of Mme. Ciolkowska. Reproduced from *Burlington Magazine*, November 1918, 176.

Although Dante and Beatrice are not mentioned in the poem, the title *La Béatrice* with its Dantesque association apparently inspired Rodin to return to an earlier drawing inscribed "*Dante et Virgile*" (Fig. 103a) and to copy the upper half of the torso of Dante for his illustration of the poet in *La Béatrice* (Fig. 103). In the illustration, Dante's expression becomes more perplexed and his hair stands on end to show the poet's "indecisive look, his wind-blown hair."

In the second illustration for *La Béatrice* (Fig. 104), the poet's beloved is shown in the company of three male figures who represent the "fiendish crowd" or "host of vicious demons." When the illustration was traced from a drawing of three men and a woman dancing (Fig. 104a), the men were transformed into satyrs by the addition of hooves and tails, while a bestial face was added to the figure on the right. The woman's profile was also changed to show a more sensual line of her breast. The drawing's transformation indicates that Rodin adhered to the duplicity of the poem, where the pristine beauty of the poet's mistress contrasts with ghoulish fiends and creates in the poet feelings of perplexity, humiliation, and vicarious titillation:

> The peerless beauty I so deeply loved,
> Sharing their laughter at my shocking plight,
> At times caressing them with lewd delight.

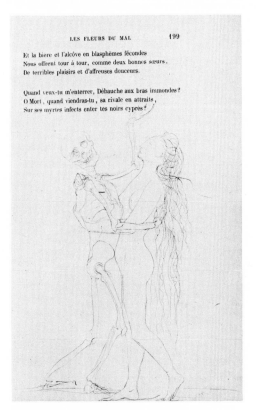

LES FLEURS DU MAL 199

Et la bière et l'alcôve en blasphèmes fécondes
Nous offrent tour à tour, comme deux bonnes sœurs,
De terribles plaisirs et d'affreuses douceurs.

Quand veux-tu m'enterrer, Débauche aux bras immondes?
O Mort, quand viendras-tu, sa rivale en attraits,
Sur ses myrtes infects enter tes noirs cyprès?

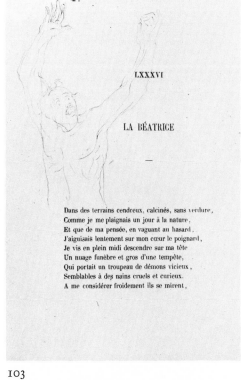

LXXXVI

LA BÉATRICE

—

Dans des terrains cendreux, calcinés, sans verdure,
Comme je me plaignais un jour à la nature,
Et que de ma pensée, en vaguant au hasard,
J'aiguisais lentement sur mon cœur le poignard,
Je vis en plein midi descendre sur ma tête
Un nuage funèbre et gros d'une tempête,
Qui portait un troupeau de démons vicieux,
Semblables à des nains cruels et curieux.
A me considérer froidement ils se mirent,

102   103

102a

103a

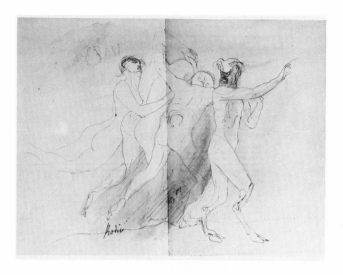

104

104a

Le globe lumineux et frêle
    Prend un grand essor,
Crève et crache son âme grêle
    Comme un songe d'or.

J'entends le crâne à chaque bulle
    Prier et gémir :
— « Ce jeu féroce et ridicule,
    Quand doit-il finir ?

Car ce que ta bouche cruelle
    Eparpille en l'air,
Monstre assassin, c'est ma cervelle,
    Mon sang et ma chair ! »

105

Mollement balancés sur l'aile
Du tourbillon intelligent,
Dans un délire parallèle,

Ma sœur, côte à côte nageant,
Nous fuirons sans repos ni trèves
Vers le Paradis de mes rêves !

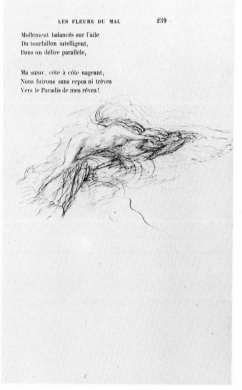

106

105 *L'Amour et le Crane* (*Cupid and the Skull*). Pen and ink. 213; 71; 228.

The most literal illustration in *Les Fleurs du Mal* was the one for *L'Amour et le Crane*, whose lines

> Astride a skull—Humanity's —
> Love sits; . . .
> He blows his bubbles, blithe and gay,
> And airily they rise —

were depicted by Rodin with a cupid standing, one foot on a skull, with his arms playfully reaching toward bubbles he has blown in the air (Fig. 105).

RELATED DRAWINGS AND SCULPTURE
NOT REPRODUCED
Although the exact prototype for the illustration is not known, there are many figures of putti which may have served as examples. Some are reproduced in this catalogue in connection with the drypoint *Love Turning the World*.

106 *Le Vin des Amants* (*The Wine of Lovers*). Pen and ink. 239; 73; 209.

In the illustration for *Le Vin des Amants* (Fig. 106), a woman floats beside the loosely defined form of a man. Sketchy lines unite their bodies and suggest the airborne drifting of the lovers' ecstatic flight:

> My sister, floating side by side,
> We, without pause, on azure streams
> Will reach the heaven of my dreams!

107 *La Mort des Pauvres* (*Death of the Destitute*). Pen and ink. 244; 75; 242.

In Rodin's illustration for *La Mort des Pauvres* (Fig. 107) the thin, naked back of a man, his body stretched upward with open arms and his head thrown back, symbolizes the poem's theme of the longing of "the poor and naked" for death or "their reward." The back view of Rodin's sculpture *The Prodigal Son* was probably the model for the illustration.

RELATED SCULPTURE NOT REPRODUCED
The Prodigal Son (back view), 1889. Bronze. H. 55 ⅛ in. (140 cm.). Musée Rodin. Reproduced in Grappe, no. 210.

108 *La Mort des Artistes* (*Death of Artists*). Pen and ink. 248; 78; 243.

108a *Two Men Holding an Escutcheon.* c. 1875–1888. Pencil, pen and ink. 5 ⅞ x 7-9/16 in. (14.9 x 19.2 cm.). MR 1974.

As the final illustration for *Les Fleurs du Mal*, Rodin chose the poem *La Mort des Artistes* which concerns a sculptor's lifelong quest for "the heart of Nature's mystery" which he thought might yield to his genius only in the face of death. Rodin may have felt that the poem was appropriate as his pesonal epitaph and as a finale for the illustrations in view of his well-known and zealous insistance on fidelity to nature in his work.

For the illustration (Fig. 108), Rodin greatly refined an earlier drawing of two nude figures holding an escutcheon (Fig. 108a) and added the inscription "*dessins commandez à Rodin par M. Gallimard 1888.*"

108a

XCIX

LA MORT DES PAUVRES

—

C'est la Mort qui console et la Mort qui fait vivre;
C'est le but de la vie, et c'est le seul espoir
Qui, divin élixir, nous monte et nous enivre,
Et nous donne le cœur de marcher jusqu'au soir;

A travers la tempête, et la neige et le givre,
C'est la clarté vibrante à notre horizon noir;
C'est l'auberge fameuse inscrite sur le livre,
Où l'on pourra manger, et dormir et s'asseoir

Il en est qui jamais n'ont connu leur Idole,
Et ces sculpteurs damnés et marqués d'un affront,
Qui vont se martelant la poitrine et le front,

N'ont qu'un espoir, étrange et sombre Capitole!
C'est que la Mort, planant comme un Soleil nouveau,
Fera s'épanouir les fleurs de leur cerveau!

—

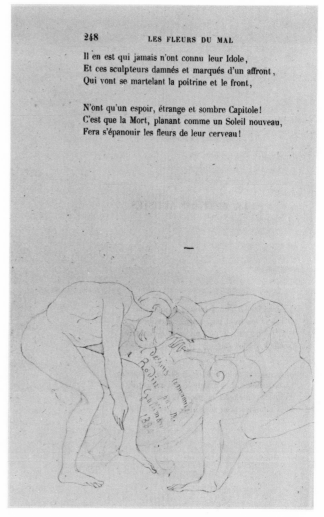

III. Octave Mirbeau.
« Le Jardin des Supplices »

Paris: Ambroise Vollard, 1902. Illustrated by Auguste
Rodin. Folio with illustrations at back, each in separate
tissue folder with text reference and reduced size reproduction
of illustration. Page size: 12¾ x 9⅞ in. (32.4 x
25.1 cm.).

Illustrations commissioned February 10, 1899; printed
1899–1900; book published May 24, 1902. One facsimile
drawing on title page (repeated on cover) and 20 original
drawings by Rodin reproduced by the lithographs of Auguste
Clot; 2 printed in black, 18 in color (green-gray contours
with one to four tints of brown, pink, orange, yellow
and green). Signed in the stone "Aug Rodin," "A. Rodin"
or "Rodin;" signature reproduced from original drawing
or signed by Clot for Rodin.

Edition of 200: 1 to 15 on Japan paper with double set of
illustrations (one in color, one with contours only); 16 to
45 on China paper with double set of illustrations (one in
color, one with contours only); 46 to 200 on vellum
(smooth ivory wove paper) by Masure and Perrigot with
watermark "Le Jardin des Supplices."

Colls: Houghton Library, Department of Printing and
Graphic Arts, Harvard University (copy no. 34); Metropolitan
Museum of Art (double set on China paper without
text); The Museum of Modern Art, Louis E. Stern Collection
(copy no. 122); New York Public Library, Spencer
Collection (copy no. 142); Philadelphia Museum of Art
(copy no. 198).

References: Delteil, nos. 13–17; Groschwitz, "The Significance
of XIX Century Color Lithography," 259–260;
Hofer, *The Artist and the Book*, 175; Johnson, *Ambroise
Vollard Editeur 1867–1939*, 136–137; Mahé, *Bibliographie des
livres de luxe de 1900 à 1928*, 955; Vollard, *Catalogue complet
des éditions Ambroise Vollard*, 14–16 and 27–28.

A contract dated February 10, 1899 between Rodin, the
author Octave Mirbeau and the publisher Ambroise Vollard
gives Vollard rights to publish 200 copies of a deluxe edition
of Mirbeau's novel *Le Jardin des Supplices*. Rodin was to
provide twenty drawings to be reproduced by the lithographer
Auguste Clot. In exchange for the rights, Rodin and
Mirbeau were to get two copies each of the deluxe edition
although the contract was later changed to give them each
four copies. The contract reads:

Between M. Vollard on the one part and Mss. Mirbeau and Rodin, on the
other part, it has been agreed as follows —
M. Mirbeau gives herewith to M. Vollard the right to publish 200 copies
of his book "Le Jardin des Supplices" which will be illustrated *hors texte*
by about twenty—this number being a minimum—original compositions
by M. Rodin made exclusively for this edition. No royalty will be due to
Mss. Mirbeau and Rodin other than two copies of "Le Jardin des Supplices"
for each of them. M. Vollard will submit for approval to M. Mirbeau the
typographic characters and it is understood that the printing of the compositions
of M. Rodin will be done by Clot. Mss. Mirbeau and Rodin
promise to sign with their initials each of the copies of "Le Jardin des Supplices."
Written in three copies in Paris, the 10th of February 1899.
Read and approved   Octave Mirbeau
Read and approved   Vollard
[left margin postscript]
The compositions of M. Rodin will be in color. Four copies instead of
two will be given to Mss. Mirbeau and Rodin. One copy will be given to
the British Museum (?) and the Museum of (?) if it does not subscribe.
[signed] Vollard. And one copy for America [signed] Vollard.
Read and approved the remarks   Octave Mirbeau. (See Appendix B,
p. 140)

At the time *Le Jardin des Supplices* was published, a letter
from Mirbeau to Rodin documented their long friendship,
one which included Mirbeau's exuberant published criticism
about Rodin's work. In the letter Mirbeau asks for an
urgent meeting to discuss *Le Jardin des Supplices* and thanks
Rodin for a photograph of himself, saying that he will keep
it "always under my eyes on my working table as the face
of my dearest friend."[1]

In Vollard's account of the publication of the book, it was
Mirbeau, rather than Rodin, who asked him to publish the
book after being turned down by other Paris publishers.
Apparently publication of the book was deemed too risky,
because it combined an avant-garde erotic novel with
drawings by Rodin, an artist who was virtually unknown
as an illustrator.[2] Mirbeau's struggle is also evident from a
critic's comment in January of 1899 that plans for the deluxe
edition had been abandoned.[3] Just a month later, however,
the contract was signed with Vollard and seven
months later, in September, receipts for drawings picked
up and returned to Rodin's studio[4] show that Clot was
printing the illustrations. Clot's work was probably finished
sometime in 1900 when the lithographs for *Le Jardin des
Supplices* were described as "perfectly traced by M. Clot for
a forthcoming deluxe edition."[5] The book itself was not
published until May 1902. In the following month Vollard
wrote Rodin that the books on China and Japan paper, the
first forty-five copies, would be ready in several days and he
would like to personally bring Rodin's copies.[6] Finally,
there is a record of Rodin thanking Vollard for receipt of
one of the promised copies over a year later in January 1903
and adding: "The pleasure that I have had of receiving it
agreeably compensates for the impatience that I have had of
possessing it."[7]

Both the contract and the book's colophon, as well as
Vollard's 1931 catalogue of his published books, name

Clot as printer of the lithographs for *Le Jardin des Supplices*. None of these sources support Delteil's statement that Rodin himself executed five of the twenty lithographs directly on the stone.[8] Delteil's statement is incorrect. There are no technical differences between the five lithographs Delteil catalogued as by Rodin's hand and those by Clot. Further, exact drawings for three of the five lithographs Delteil attributed to Rodin (Figs. 123, 129, 131) and eight of the other fifteen by Clot (Figs. 120, 121, 124, 125, 126, 128, 132, 133) are found at the Musée Rodin. That all eleven drawings were accurately transferred to the stone, with similar and tiny deviations from the original drawings such as a more even tone at the border of a wash, indicates the hand of a professional lithographer rather than an original artist. Clot's skill was compared to the best seventeenth- and eighteenth-century reproductive engravers,[9] and he was described as one of Rodin's talented "collaborators" able to reproduce the sculptor's drawings so well that the "master could scarcely discern the originals."[10] There is a remarkably accurate correspondence between the drawings for *Le Jardin des Supplices* and the lithographs. Vollard quotes Rodin's comment on the *Le Jardin des Supplices* lithographs: "I did them with Clot. When he is gone, lithography will be a lost art."[11]

The drawings for *Le Jardin des Supplices* are contour sketches drawn from the natural gestures of a posed or moving model. The drawings have been simplified and refined through tracing, many of them going through several versions (Figs. 119a, 123a, 123b). This simplified mode of the late drawing style (1896–1917) was chosen for the illustrations instead of (1) the artist's initial, direct sketches of a model in which there were usually more irregular and multiple lines (Figs. 119a, 123b), or (2) his drawings of a model (either the first sketches or a refined, traced version) which had been subsequently transformed by adding washes, *estompe*, lines of emphasis, suggestive inscriptions or symbolic objects such as a snake.

Five preparatory drawings found for *Le Jardin des Supplices* show that Rodin considered illustrating specific scenes from the text. All five are ordinary gesture drawings overlaid with a complex iconography of torture and eroticism. On the drawing of a seated woman, Rodin added a spike through her foot and a cross behind it; he tinted the figure's hair and crotch with red-brown shades of blood, and inscribed "*jardin des supplices*" and "*japonais*," alluding to a Japanese torture (Fig. 109). In a second drawing, Rodin inscribed "*Mirbeau/ theatre . . . (?)*" on the erotic drawing of a model lying on her back facing the viewer with her legs in the air.[12]

A model reclining languidly with one arm seductively raised behind her head was inscribed "*Mirbeau massacre*" and blood-red wash was mingled with chaotic and forcefully applied lines to suggest a massacre described by Mirbeau (Fig. 110). While none of these drawings were adopted for the final illustrations, a variant version of one preparatory drawing inscribed "*jardin des supplices*" (Fig. 114a) was included as the frontispiece (Fig. 114). The drawing represents a woman's torso which Rodin had often abstracted and compared in his inscriptions and statements to a Greek vase form.[13] Here, however, it was given an erotic connotation by a snake coiled around the woman's waist and redoubled into a phallic shape. In the frontispiece, this meaning was suppressed with the omission of the snake and by the selection of a version of the torso where the model's head was tilted backward so that her chin became the peak of a highly abstract form.

A fifth drawing of a reclining woman with one arm outstretched (Fig. 111), to which a wheel of torture and the word "*torture*" has been added may represent the artist's recollection (at the time of the Mirbeau illustrations) of the theme of torture which he had treated in an earlier drawing. In the earlier composition (c. 1864–1875), a male nude also lies on his back with one arm outstretched, beneath a wheel of torture (Fig. 112). The closely-knit early composition presents a clear contrast to the artist's late period practice of sketching the model's gesture first and later allowing it to suggest to him such a fantastic connotation as torture.

Rodin's iconographic addenda created ambiguous and suggestive images in the spirit of the intuitive symbolists of the late nineteenth century. Among Rodin's motives for choosing his refined, traced mode for the *Le Jardin des Supplices* illustrations—omitting the inscriptions, the wheel of torture, the nail and cross, and the snake girdle—may have been the recognition that the line of Mirbeau's text to which each illustration was keyed was sufficient suggestion for the reader's imagination. It is also possible that the preparatory drawings were not appropriate to passages ultimately chosen, or that these drawings were considered too overtly erotic. Another consideration may have been that the simplified mode was easier for Clot to transfer to the stone.

While it is not known whether Rodin or Mirbeau keyed the drawings to the text, the drawings and text complement each other and create an evocative blend. On the most universal level, the lascivious passages of Mirbeau have an immediate resonance with Rodin's drawings of nude women. In the general context of *Le Jardin des Supplices*,

Rodin's embracing women can be seen as Lesbian lovers and his frank and unusual views of the female nude as embodying the infinite stirring and diversity of sexual feelings described by Mirbeau.

The reader may also choose to view the illustrations and text in closer proximity. In the novel, the narrator, a petty French deputy sent to a new post in China after a scandal in his home office meets Clara, an eccentric Englishwoman, on board the ship. Their affair takes him into the depths of depravity which culminates in a tour of a Chinese torture garden, a travesty which metaphorically blends the novel's themes of political satire and *fin de siècle* eroticism.

Rodin's first seven illustrations for the novel follow the *femme fatale* Clara as she lures her prey: Clara strokes her hair (Fig. 116), tempts with her body (Figs. 118, 119), and relates prurient fantasies from her past affairs with women (Figs. 115, 117, 120, 121). The next five illustrations are views from the torture garden. The first (Fig. 122) gives substance to the executioner's boast that he can make a man's body out of a woman's corpse; the phallic shape of watercolor at the woman's pubis with its accidental origin and subsequent interpretation accords with Rodin's treatment of the theme of the hermaphrodite in other late drawings.[14] The cunning legerdemain of the executioner is symbolized by the artist's drawing of a male nude gymnast turned upside down so that his body seems to parachute through the air (Fig. 123). Rodin's drawing of a crawling woman illustrates a torture where a rat is hermetically applied (Fig. 124), and the drawing of a seated woman with arms together above her head is keyed to the line "She was suspended by her wrists from an iron hook" (Fig. 125). At the end of the day in the torture garden, "Shadow descends on the garden . . .;" Rodin symbolized nightfall by the bowed figure of a woman surrounded by a circle, rays and the yellow color of the sun (Fig. 126). His subsequent interpretation of a model's rising, leaping or bowing gestures as symbolic of the movement of the sun was often noted in his late drawings by affixing sun symbols and appropriate inscriptions.[15] As twilight falls, Clara exits the torture garden, her supple movements symbolized by the drawing of a sinuous nude woman (Fig. 127).

The last six illustrations record Clara's death: "the fleeting scenes of wild debauchery" around her are represented by the drawing of a woman with her legs apart, one hand at her crotch (Fig. 128); her death spasms ("legs tense and vibrant as the strings of a viol") are symbolized by the elongated body of a woman lying stretched out viewed from above (Fig. 129); the caresses and tender words of the Chinese woman attendant ("Little, little friend of my

breasts and my soul . . .") are alluded to in the drawing of Lesbian lovers (Fig. 130); Clara's notoriety spread at her death ". . . like some monstrous obscenity" is personified by a seated nude with one arm behind her head in the seduction or prostitute's gesture (Fig. 131); death's last spasms where ". . . the demons must leave her body" are portrayed by a woman's body arched up as she crawls on all fours (Fig. 132); and finally, death's agony over Clara, who "seemed to be returning from a long and agonizing sleep," is a subterranean vision evoked by Rodin's drawing of a model bending over, her head and lower body covered with transparent green watercolor (Fig. 133).

1. Undated letter from Octave Mirbeau to Rodin, Musée Rodin archives, Mirbeau folder. The mention of *Le Jardin des Supplices* could refer to either the 1902 edition or an earlier edition of 1899 which used a Rodin drawing as the frontispiece. See section on Rodin's frontispieces in this catalogue.

2. Vollard, *Catalogue complet*, 14.

3. F. Fague, "Ses Collaborateurs," *La Revue des Beaux-Arts et des Lettres*, 13. ". . . on en pourra voir cependant illustrer la prochaine édition de luxe du Jardin des Supplices d'Octave Mirbeau mais par accident: les Rodins de M. Clot ne sont pas non plus destinés au commerce."

4. Receipt dated September 30, 1899, Paris, and signed by Clot. Musée Rodin archives, A. Clot folder. "Sur 24 dessins reçus. Remis ce jour à Monsieur Rodin 14 dessins. Reste à Monsieur Clot 10 dessins dont Cinq dessins en tirage pr. (?) Le Jardin des Supplices et Cinq dessins en reproduction. Clot."

5. Riotor, *Auguste Rodin, Statuaire*, 26: "Il accorda un prelude au Jardin des Supplices, d'Octave Mirbeau, et des originaux parfaitement calqués par M. Clot, pour une édition de luxe prochaine de cet ouvrage."

6. Letter dated June 28, 1902, from Vollard to Rodin, Musée Rodin archives, Vollard folder. "Cher Monsieur Rodin, j'apprend par Clot avec le plus grand plaisir que vous êtes rendu (?) à Paris, je ne serrais de demander à tous les échos de vos nouvelles et personne me pourrait m'en donner. Je serai très heureux de vous voir afin de vous porter moi même des exemplaires du Jardin des Supplices. Je n'aurai que dans deux ou trois jours tout à qu'il faut pour avoir mes exemplaires chine et japon complet. Voudriez vous me donner un rendez-vous à partir de mercredi prochaine que je puisse vous porter moi même des exemplaires, avec mes salutations les plus . . . (?) Vollard, 6 rue Laffit."

7. Letter dated January 30, 1903 from 182, Rue de l'Université, Print Department, Staatsgalerie Stuttgart. "Monsieur Vollard, / Recevez mes remerciments pour l'exemplaire du Jardin des Supplices. Le plaisir que j'ai à l'avoir compense agréablement l'impatience que j'avais de le possède. Recevez je vous prie me bien cordiales salutations. A Rodin."

8. Delteil, no. 13–17. "L'ouvrage contient vingt lithographies; mais en réalité, cinq seulement ont été exécutées directement sur pierre [emphasis Delteil's] par le maître-statuaire."

9. A. Mellerio, "Les Dessins de Rodin, interpretés lithographiquement en couleurs, par A. Clot," *La Plume*, special issue devoted to Rodin, 1900, 82.

10. Fague, "Ses Collaborateurs," 13.

11. A. Vollard, *Auguste Renoir*, Paris: Les Editions G. Cres et Cie., 1920, 209.

12. *Nude Woman with Her Legs in the Air*. c. 1899. Pencil and watercolor. 12¾ x 9½ in. (32.5 x 24.1 cm.). MR 4034.

13. For a discussion of the Greek vase iconography in Rodin's late drawings see V. Thorson, "Symbolism and Conservatism in Rodin's Late Drawings," in Elsen and Varnedoe, *The Drawings of Rodin*, 126–127.

14. The iconography of the hemaphrodite is discussed in Thorson, *The Late Drawings of Auguste Rodin*, 155–158.

15. Rodin's sun symbolism is explained in *ibid.*, 137–143.

109 *Woman Nailed to Cross.* 1899. Pencil and watercolor.
12¾ x 9¾ in. (32.4 x 24.8 cm.). Inscribed "*Jardin des Supplices / japonais.*" MR 4258.

110 *Mirbeau Massacre.* 1899. Pencil and watercolor. 9¾ x
12⅞ in. (24.8 x 32.7 cm.). Inscribed "*Mirbeau massacre.*"
MR 5030.

109

110

111   *Woman with Wheel of Torture*. 1899. Pencil and water-color. 12¾ x 9¾ in. (32.4 x 24.8 cm.). Inscribed *"torture."* MR 3953.

112   *Man under Wheel of Torture*. c. 1864–1875. Charcoal, pen and ink. 3-15/16 x 5⅞ in. (10 x 14.9 cm.). MR 433.

113   Cover and title page for *Le Jardin des Supplices*. 12¾ x 9⅞ in. (32.4 x 25.1 cm.). Philadelphia Museum of Art. Facsimile of a drawing traced from *Bending Woman* (reproduced in Roger-Marx, "Rodin Ressenateur et Graveur," 354).

114   Frontispiece for *Le Jardin des Supplices*. Lithograph by Clot after a Rodin drawing. 12¾ x 9⅞ in. (32.4 x 25.1 cm.). Philadelphia Museum of Art.*

114a   *Woman Engirded by Snake*. 1899. Pencil and water-color. 12¾ x 9⅜ in. (32.4 x 23.8 cm.). Inscribed *"Jardin des Supplices."* MR 1530.

* Subsequent illustrations are keyed to a line from *Le Jardin des Supplices*. The line and page number will be given in each caption; information about the medium, page size and collection, which are the same for all, will be omitted. Related works will be numbered as Fig. 114a, etc.

115   *"Jamais plus nous ne connaîtrons le goût si âpre de ses baisers! . . ."* ("Never again will we know the bitter taste of her kisses! . . ."), 2.

116   *"Avec des gestes lents et charmants, Clara lissa l'or roux de ses cheveux."* ("With slow and charming gestures, Clara smoothed the red-gold of her hair."), 5.

117   *"Une splendide créature que j'avais aimée la veille."* ("A splendid creature [a woman] whom I [Clara] had loved the night before."), 9.

117a   *Two Nude Women Facing Each Other*. 1899. Pencil and watercolor. 17¼ x 11¾ in. (43.8 x 29.8 cm.). Inscribed *"Le Fort . . . (?)"* MR 5051. Same two figures as in lithograph but positions vertically closer together; both compositions created by arranging cut-out figures and tracing them. Lower figure also in group of three cut-out figures glued on sheet 22½ x 28½ in. (57.1 x 72.4 cm.). Princeton University Library. Reproduced in Varnedoe, *The Drawings of Rodin*, fig. 89.

118   *"Tu ne diras pas cela, ce soir, quand tu seras dans mes bras . . . et que je t'aimerai! . . ."* ("You won't say that tonight, when you are in my arms . . . and when I love you! . . ."), 29.

111

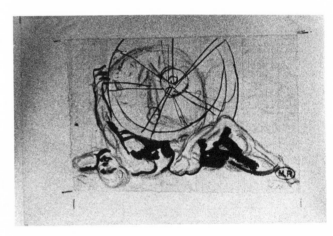

112

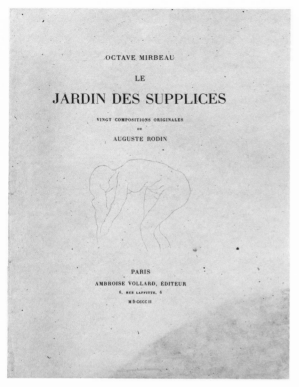

113

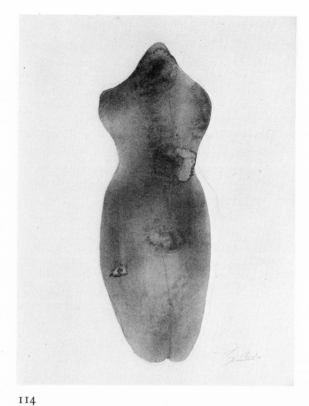

114

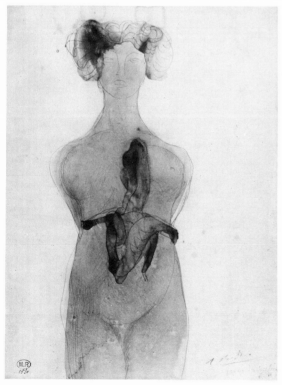

114a

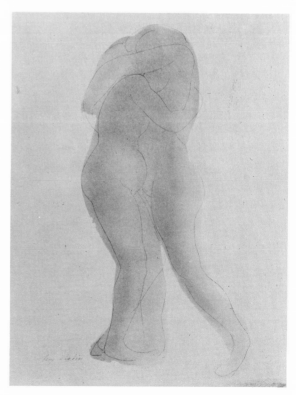

115

116

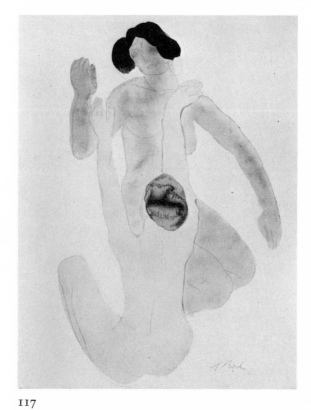

117

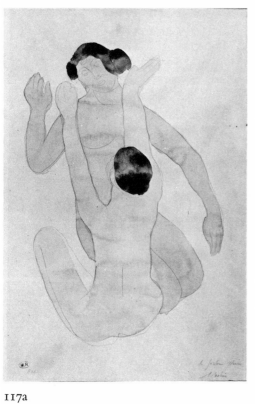

117a

118

119 *"Caresse-moi donc, chéri! . . . tâte comme mes seins sont froids et durs."* ("Caress me, darling! . . . Feel how cold and firm my breasts are."), 30. (Reproduced in Delteil, no. 17.)
119a *Back View of Kneeling Woman.* c. 1899. Pencil and small spots of red watercolor. 10¼ x 8 in. (26 x 20.3 cm.). Inscribed *"bas."* MR 523. Related drawing not reproduced: *Back View of Kneeling Woman with Snake,* c. 1899–1905, pencil and watercolor, 12⅝ x 9¾ in. (32 x 24.8 cm.), inscribed *"serpent et ève."* MR 3945.

120 *"La seconde a une abondante chevelure qui brille et se déroule en longues guirlandes de soie."* ("The second has abundant hair which gleams and flows in long silky garlands."), 46. Drawing for the lithograph not reproduced: *Seated Woman,* c. 1899, pencil and watercolor, 12-11/16 x 9-11/16 in. (32.2 x 24.6 cm.). MR 3931.

121 *"Et c'est celle-là que j'aime."* ("And she is the one I love."), 47. Drawing for the lithograph not reproduced: *Nude Woman,* c. 1899, pencil and watercolor, 12½ x 9¾ in. (31.8 x 24. 8 cm.) (mat opening). MR 4330.

122 *"Demain, si les génies veulent bien m'accorder la grâce que j'aie une femme, à ce gibet . . . j'en ferai un homme . . ."* ("Tomorrow, if the genii grant me a woman on this gibbet . . . I'll make a man of her. . ."), 81.

123 *"Et pourtant, dit-il, moi qui vous parle Milady . . . je ne suis pas le premier venu."* ("And besides, he said, I who speak to you milady . . . I'm certainly not just anybody."), 86. (Reproduced in Delteil, no. 14.)
123a *Male Acrobat.* 1899. Pencil and watercolor (brown-yellow flesh and black hair, same tones as lithograph). 12¾ x 9¾ in. (32.4 x 24.8 cm.). Inscribed *"souffle."* Signature stamp "Rodin." MR 4953.
123b *Acrobat in Motion.* c. 1896–1899. Pencil. 12⅝ x 8¾ in. (32.2 x 21.2 cm.). MR 1310.

124 *"Vous mettez un très gros rat, qu'il convient d'avoir privé de nourriture. . ."* ("You place a very fat rat, whom it is wise to have deprived of nourishment. . ."), 88. Drawing for the lithograph not reproduced: *Kneeling Woman,* c. 1899, pencil and watercolor (same tone of dark brown as lithograph), 11-11/16 x 17⅜ in. (29.7 x 44.1 cm.). MR 6362.

125 *"Elle était suspendue, par les poignets, à un crochet de fer."* ("She was suspended by her wrists from an iron hook."), 131.

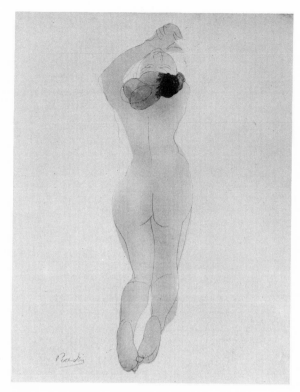

119

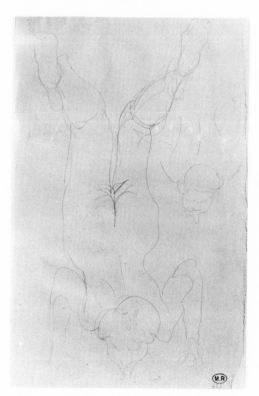

119a

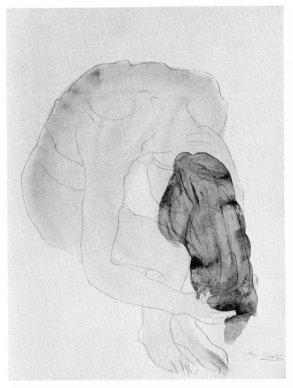

120

121

122

123

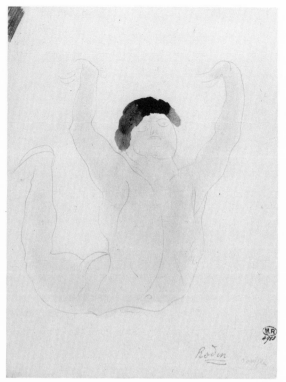

123a

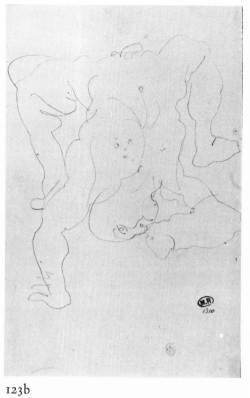

123b

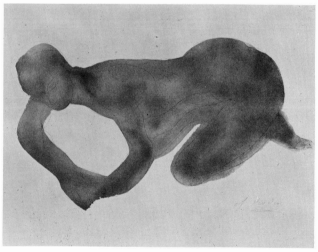

124

125

125a   *Seated Woman with Arms above Head.* 1899. Pencil and watercolor. 12½ x 9⅝ in. (31.8 x 24.4 cm.). Inscribed ". . . (?) *des bras.*" Signed "Aug Rodin." MR 4609.
125b   *Seated Female Nude.* c. 1899–1905. Pencil and pink watercolor. 12¾ x 9-13/16 in. (32.4 x 24.9 cm.). Signed "A Rodin." The Art Institute of Chicago.

126   "*L'ombre descend sur le jardin. . .*" ("Shadow descends on the garden. . ."), 137.
126a   *Nude Woman as Sun Symbol.* 1899. Pencil and water-color (flesh color, brown hair, and yellow sun). 9⅝ x 12-9/16 in. (24.4 x 31.9 cm.). Inscribed "*la chute du jour de la gloire / appallon (?) cassé (?).*" Signed "A Rodin." MR 4711.

127   "*Et telle est-l'invulnérable beauté de son corps. . .*" ("And such is the invulnerable beauty of her body. . ."), 142.

128   "*A peine si, par les hublots et les fenêtres éclairées, je pus voir—visions rapides—des débauches hurlantes. . .*" ("Through portholes and lighted windows I caught fleeting scenes of wild debauchery. . ."), 151. Drawing for the lithograph not reproduced: *Seated Woman,* 1899, pencil and water-color, 9¾ x 12¾ in. (24.8 x 32.5 cm.), signed at left "Aug Rodin" (lithograph signed by Clot at right). MR 4085.

125b

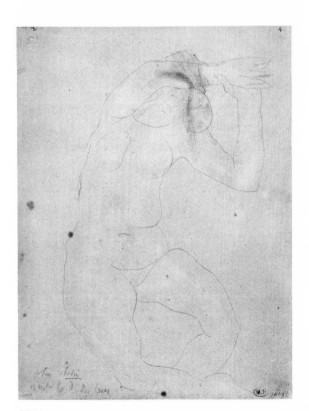

125a

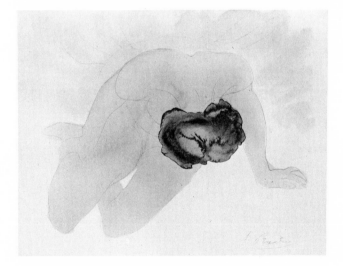

126

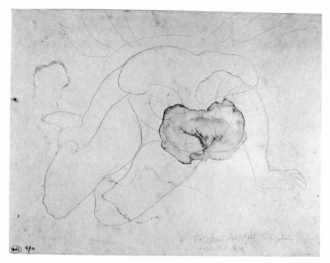

126a

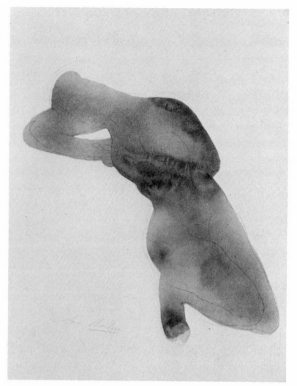

127

128

129   "*Les jambes tendues et vibrantes ainsi que les cordes d'une
viole . . .*" ("Her legs tense and vibrant as the strings of a
viole . . ."), 151. (Reproduced in Delteil, no. 15.) Drawing
for the lithograph not reproduced: *Reclining Nude Seen from
Above*, 1899, pencil, MR 1430 (reproduced in Charles
Morice, *Rodin*, Paris: H. Floury, 1900, 7).
129a   *Nude Woman Lying on Her Stomach.* c. 1899–1905.
Pencil and watercolor (flesh color, black hair, blue background). 12¾ x 8½ in. (32.4 x 21.6 cm.). Inscribed
"*marbre* / . . . (?)" MR 4942.

129

130 "*Petite, petite amie de mes seins et de mon âme . . . que vous êtes belle ainsi! . . .*" ("Little, little friend of my breasts and my soul . . . how beautiful you are like that! . . ."), 155.

131 "*Et le nom de Clara, chuchoté de lèvres en lèvres, de lit en lit, de chambre en chambre, emplit bientôt le bateau de fleurs comme une obscénité merveilleuse.*" ("And Clara's name, whispered from mouth to mouth, from bed to bed, and room to room, soon filled the flower-boat like a marvelous obscenity."), 158. (Reproduced in Delteil, no. 16.)

131a *Seated Nude with One Arm Behind Head*. 1899. Pencil and watercolor. 12⅝ x 9⅞ in. (32 x 25 cm.) (mat opening). MR 4528.

132 "*Car il faut que les démons s'en aillent de son corps. . . .*" ("For the demons must leave her body. . . ."), 163. Drawing for the lithograph not reproduced: *Woman on All Fours*, 1899, pencil and watercolor, 9¾ x 12¾ in. (24.8 x 32.4 cm.). MR 4707.

133 "*Elle semblait revenir d'un long, d'un angoissant sommeil. . . .*" ("She seemed to be returning from a long and agonizing sleep. . . ."), 163.

133a *Nude Woman Bending Over*. 1899. Pencil and watercolor. 17½ x 12 in. (44.4 x 30.5 cm.). MR 4592.

129a

130

131

131a

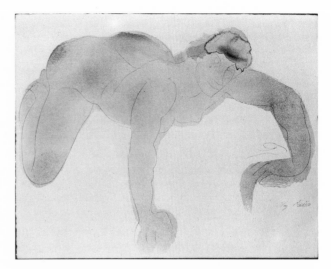

132

133

133a

IV. « Les Elégies amoureuses d'Ovide »

Paris: Philippe Gonin, 1935. Translated into French verse by Abbé Bazzin. Preface by Georges Grappe. Illustrated by Auguste Rodin. Folio format with partial page illustrations on same page as text; a few full page illustrations. Page size: 11 x 7½ in. (28 x 19 cm.).

Illustrations conceived around 1900, according to Grappe. Book published posthumously, December 7, 1935; 31 original drawings by Rodin interpreted into wood engravings by J. L. Perrichon. Signature stamp "Aug Rodin." Pencil signature "J. L. Perrichon" on a few illustrations.

Edition of 250: 1 to 50 on pure hemp Maillol paper (first few copies, of an unspecified number, include wood engraved portrait of Rodin by Perrichon); 51 to 250 on pure rag of Montval; 20 additional copies numbered in Roman numerals on Maillol paper, not for sale; 25 additional copies on China paper.

Colls: Bibliothèque Nationale (includes portrait of Rodin by Perrichon); New York Public Library, Spencer Collection.

References: Grappe, "Ovide et Rodin," 203–208; Hofer, *The Artist and the Book*, 175.

Whether Rodin intended to illustrate an edition of Ovid and whether he would have considered the posthumous edition *Les Elégies amoureuses d'Ovide*, published in 1935, as a book illustrated by his hand is not known with certainty. One cannot rule out the possibility that the book was conceived and executed by the publisher Philippe Gonin, the wood engraver J. L. Perrichon who could have used existing and newly cut wood blocks, and the then *conservateur* of the Musée Rodin, Georges Grappe, who wrote the preface and who had access to Rodin's vast store of drawings. If we accept Grappe's representations in the preface, however, Rodin and Perrichon first conceived of an edition of Ovid about 1900 to be illustrated with a selection of Perrichon's best wood engravings made after Rodin's drawings, although the project was never realized during Rodin's lifetime. Grappe tells us that the young wood engraver first met Rodin in 1898, frequented Rodin's home at Meudon around 1900, and started to do reproductive wood engravings of Rodin's drawings at that time. This is documented by a series of fifteen wood engravings of the sculptor's drawings published in the special issue of *La Plume* dedicated to Rodin in 1900. Three more woodcuts that appeared in publications in 1903 (Figs. 146, 156) and 1909 (Fig. 166) were included as well in the 1935 Ovid illustrations. The fact that the 1903 and 1909 reproductions, with their greater fluidity and improved technique, were chosen for the Ovid

may support Grappe's statement that a selection of the best reproductions was to be used, although it is not clear whether Rodin earmarked them for the edition during his lifetime.

As faithful reproductions of Rodin's drawings, Perrichon's woodcuts are inferior in quality to the facsimile reproductions by photogravure for *Enguerrande* and *Les Fleurs du Mal* or the transfer lithographs of Clot for *Le Jardin des Supplices*. However, the colophon of *Les Elégies amoureuses d'Ovide* reminds us that it "is composed of 31 original compositions by Auguste Rodin interpreted in wood engraving by J. L. Perrichon," and an interpretation would allow for the simplifications and stylizations of the wood engraver. The distance of Perrichon's woodcuts from Rodin's original drawings is analogous to the interpretations which crept into the marbles cut by his workshop as contrasted with the more faithful translations of Rodin's clay models when plaster or bronze casts were made. Just as Rodin had his own aesthetic and commercial motives for wanting to see his work translated into marble, he had also asked Perrichon to transpose his drawings into wood engravings. Grappe provides the plausible explanation that Rodin complained to Perrichon "of the softness that the printing process was giving to his work [drawings]." The same composition used in two slightly varying versions for both the Ovid and *Le Jardin des Supplices* provides a chance to compare Rodin's original drawings (Figs. 125a and 161a) with the reproductions of Clot (Fig. 125) and Perrichon (Fig. 161). It is true that Clot's lithographs, though extremely faithful to the originals, do not show the variations in pressure and acuity of a Rodin line and tend to appear slightly flatter in tone than the originals. On the other hand, the broken, less accurate lines of Perrichon's wood engravings, which remained raised after the rest of the block was cut away, did, when inked and printed, appear bolder than lines reproduced by lithography or photogravure.

Many of Rodin's original drawings that were used for the Ovid have been found at the Musée Rodin (Figs. 146a, 150a, 153b, 161a, 163a). Several of Perrichon's tracings for the woodblocks, done on thin paper with pin holes along the margins (Fig. 140a; see captions for Figs. 135, 139, 157, 158, 161, 165), and some proofs or separate prints of Ovid illustrations (Fig. 153a; see caption for Fig. 148) have been found in U.S. collections. A comparison of Rodin's originals with the Perrichon tracings and wood engravings reveals the changes made by the engraver and provides a basis for recognizing his hand. In general, Perrichon normalized more unusual proportions and distortions characteristic of Rodin's late drawings made directly from a moving or arrested model. If there were several contours,

Perrichon chose one or traced his line in between, and he often changed facial gestures, hair, or hands to give them his own stylizations.

Iconographically, all of the drawings for the Ovid illustrations are of the model in natural, relaxed poses, either standing, sitting, or reclining, and either completely nude or covered only with a simple sleeveless tunic, often carelessly pulled up around her waist to expose her legs and hips. An unusual inscription on one drawing of a reclining model wearing a tunic (Fig. 134) whose pose is very close to two of the Ovid figures may indicate Rodin's intention to illustrate the edition of Ovid. While most inscriptions on Rodin's drawings are either derived from the traditional metaphors of history, mythology and literature or refer to his highly personal fantasies, there are a few notations about his work for sculpture or, in this case, for a group of drawings. Although it is only a possibility, the words "*Chanson de geste pour tous les dessins*," translated as "song (or verse-chronicle) for all the drawings," may be Rodin's notation that the model's gesture was to set the tone or style for a suite of drawings which could have been the Ovid illustrations.

134 *Reclining Woman*. c. 1900. Pencil and watercolor. 9⅝ x 12⅝ in. (24.4 x 32 cm.). Inscribed "*Chanson de geste pour tous les dessins*." MR 5660.

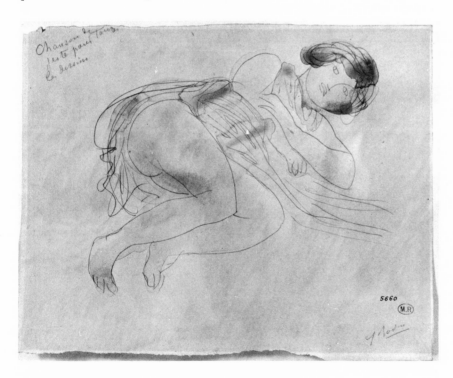

135   Title page for *Les Elégies amoureuses d'Ovide*. c. 1900.
Wood engraving by J. L. Perrichon after a Rodin drawing.
11 x 7½ in. (28 x 19 cm.). Bibliothèque Nationale.*
135a   *Seated Woman*. c. 1900. Pencil and watercolor.
12⅝ x 9-13/16 in. (32 x 24.9 cm.). Signed "Rodin."
MR 5003. Related drawings not reproduced: *Two Women,
One Seated*, c. 1900, pencil, 12-13/16 x 7-11/16 in. (31 x
19.5 cm.), MR 1341; and a tracing by J. L. Perrichon:
Seated Woman, c. 1900, ink over pencil, 15¼ x 10⅜ in.
(38.7 x 26.4 cm.), collection of Mr. and Mrs. Charles J.
Solomon, Philadelphia (reproduced in Elsen, *Rodin*, 164).

136   *Les Elégies amoureuses d'Ovide*, 5.

137   *Les Elégies amoureuses d'Ovide*, 9.
137a   *Woman Reposing*. c. 1900–1905. Pencil. 7⅝ x
11-15/16 in. (19.4 x 30.3 cm.). Signed "Aug Rodin." The
Metropolitan Museum of Art, Rogers Fund, 1910.

   * Captions for subsequent illustrations will include only the title *Les
Elégies amoureuses d'Ovide* and the page number of the illustration. The date,
medium and collection, which remain the same throughout, will be
omitted. Related works will be numbered as Fig. 135a, etc.

135

135a

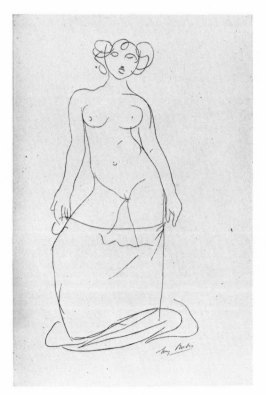

136

137

137a

123

138   *Les Elégies amoureuses d'Ovide*, 11.

139   *Les Elégies amoureuses d'Ovide*, 13. Tracing by J. L.
Perrichon not reproduced: *Woman Leaning Back*, c. 1900,
pencil on tracing paper with pin holes along edges of paper,
12 7/8 x 9 in. (32.7 x 22.9 cm.), Philadelphia Museum of Art.

140   *Les Elégies amoureuses d'Ovide*, 15.
140a   *Seated Figure with Arms Raised*. c. 1900. Tracing by
J. L. Perrichon. Pencil on tracing paper with pin holes
along edges of paper. 13 x 10½ in. (33 x 26.7 cm.). Philadelphia Museum of Art.

141   *Les Elégies amoureuses d'Ovide*, 21.

142   *Les Elégies amoureuses d'Ovide*, 26.
142a   *Lightly Draped Dancing Female Nude*. c. 1900–1905.
Pencil. 12 1/8 x 7¾ in. (30.7 x 19.8 cm.). Inscribed "*hommage
affectueux à Madame C. Steichen / Aug Rodin*." Courtesy of
The Art Institute of Chicago.

138

139

140

140a

141

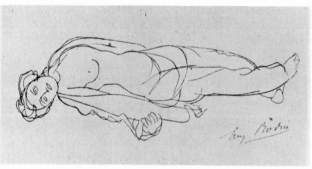

142

142a

143   *Les Elégies amoureuses d'Ovide*, 28.

144   *Les Elégies amoureuses d'Ovide*, 31.
144a   *Nude Torso*. c. 1900. Pencil and watercolor, cut-out figure. H. of figure: 11¼ in. (28.6 cm.). MR 5265.

145   *Les Elégies amoureuses d'Ovide*, 36. Tracing not reproduced: *Woman Reclining with Legs Apart*, c. 1900, pencil, 7⅞ x 12¼ in. (20 x 31.1 cm.). MR 2828.

146   *Les Elégies amoureuses d'Ovide*, 39. (Reproduced in *Les Maîtres Artistes*, between 308 and 309.)
146a   *Seated Woman Wearing Chemise*. c. 1900. Tracing in pencil and watercolor. 12⅝ x 9⅝ in. (32 x 24.4 cm.). Signed "A Rodin." MR 5056.

147   *Les Elégies amoureuses d'Ovide*, 41.

143

144

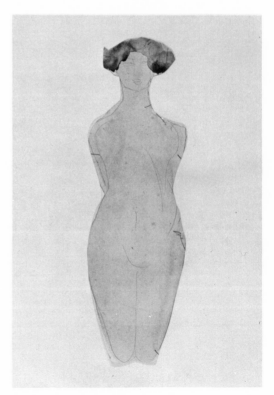

144a

145

146

146a

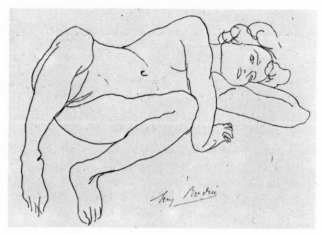

147

148 *Les Elégies amoureuses d'Ovide*, 45. Separate wood
engraving not reproduced: 3¼ x 5¼ in. (8.2 x 13.3 cm.),
signed in pencil "J. L. Perrichon S.L.," collection unknown,
formerly Collection Mr. and Mrs. Charles J. Solomon,
Philadelphia.

149 *Les Elégies amoureuses d'Ovide*, 47.

150 *Les Elégies amoureuses d'Ovide*, 48.
150a *Standing Nude Seen from Back.* c. 1900. Tracing in
pencil. 12¼ x 7½ in. (31.1 x 19 cm.). Signed "A Rodin."
MR 871.

151 *Les Elégies amoureuses d'Ovide*, 51.

152 *Les Elégies amoureuses d'Ovide*, 55.

149

148

150

150a

151

152

153 *Les Elégies amoureuses d'Ovide*, 57.
153a Separate wood engraving. 5¼ x 3¼ in. (13.3 x
8.3 cm.). Signed in pencil "J. L. Perrichon S.L." Collection
Mr. and Mrs. Charles J. Solomon, Philadelphia.
153b *Nude Woman Kneeling.* c. 1896–1900. Tracing in
pencil. 12¼ x 8 in. (31.1 x 20.3 cm.). MR 775.

154 *Les Elégies amoureuses d'Ovide*, 59. Tracing not reproduced: *Kneeling Woman Wearing Chemise*, c. 1896–1900,
pencil, MR 2606.

155 *Les Elégies amoureuses d'Ovide*, 61.

156 *Les Elégies amoureuses d'Ovide*, 64. (Reproduced in
Les Maîtres Artistes, between 276 and 277.)

157 *Les Elégies amoureuses d'Ovide*, 67. Tracing not repro-
duced: *Seated Woman Wearing Chemise*, c. 1900, pencil,
MR 2575; tracing by J. L. Perrichon not reproduced: *Seated
Woman Wearing Chemise*, c. 1900, pen and ink, 11¾ x
7⅛ in. (30 x 18 cm.), Collection Mr. and Mrs. Laurence
Brunswick, Rydal, Pennsylvania.

153

153a

153b

154

155

156

157

158 *Les Elégies amoureuses d'Ovide*, 69. Tracing not reproduced: *Standing Woman, Back View with Chemise*, c. 1900,
pencil, MR 5134; tracing by J. L. Perrichon not reproduced:
Woman, Back View with Chemise, c. 1900, pencil, pen and
ink, 14½ x 7½ in. (37 x 19 cm.), Collection Mr. and Mrs.
Charles J. Solomon, Philadelphia.

159 *Les Elégies amoureuses d'Ovide*, 72. Related drawing
not reproduced: *Kneeling Nude with Arms Behind Back*,
c. 1900–1905, pencil and watercolor, 12½ x 10½ in. (31.8 x
26.7 cm.), inscribed *"ange précipice / Rodin,"* Maryhill
Museum of Fine Arts, Maryhill, Washington.

160 *Les Elégies amoureuses d'Ovide*, 74.

161 *Les Elégies amoureuses d'Ovide*, 77. Tracing by J. L.
Perrichon not reproduced: *Seated Woman with Arms above
Head*, c. 1899, pen and ink (white gouache along some contours), on indefinite loan to Yale University Art Gallery.
161a *Seated Woman with Arms above Head*. c. 1899. Tracing
in pencil. MR 1263.

158

159

160

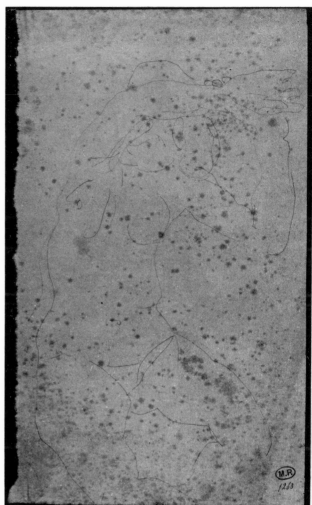

161

161a

162   *Les Elégies amoureuses d'Ovide*, 79.

163   *Les Elégies amoureuses d'Ovide*, 82.

163a   *Kneeling Draped Woman with Arms Raised*. c. 1900. Tracing in pencil. 12¾ x 9⅞ in. (32.4 x 25 cm.). Inscribed "*après la prière*." MR 7178. (Reproduced in Cladel, *Auguste Rodin, l'œuvre et l'homme*, opp. 130.)

164   *Les Elégies amoureuses d'Ovide*, 87. Tracing not reproduced: *Seated Female Nude with Legs Tucked under Her*, c. 1900, pencil, 7¾ x 12¼ in. (19.7 x 31.1 cm.), inscribed "*Virgile aux champs Elysées*," MR 1223.

162

163

163a

164

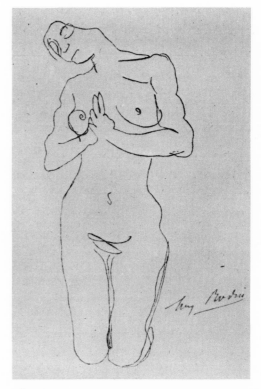

165

165   *Les Elégies amoureuses d'Ovide*, 91. Tracing by J. L.
Perrichon not reproduced: *Kneeling Nude with Hands
Clasped in Front*, c. 1896–1900, pen and ink, 13-3/16 x
9-7/16 in. (33.8 x 24 cm.), Collection of Mr. and Mrs.
Laurence Brunswick, Rydal, Pennsylvania.

166   *Les Elégies amoureuses d'Ovide*, 93. (Reproduced in
Rudolf Dircks, *Auguste Rodin*, London: Siegle, Hill & Co.,
1909.)

166

Frontispieces

In 1900 Léon Riotor, whose biography of Rodin included a frontispiece, facsimile of the drypoint *The Dying Centaur*, mentioned as well that "one can see at Rodin's an innumerable suite of portraits and of frontispieces for many works of friends."[1] The remark is borne out by Rodin's two frontispieces for his friend Octave Mirbeau, one for the critic and his supporter Gustave Geffroy, and the one for Léon Riotor's biography. An additional frontispiece, of a different type, was provided for a volume of Victor Hugo's poems and was actually a wood engraving by J. L. Perrichon after Rodin's bust of *Victor Hugo* from the Victor Hugo Monument. A final illustration which further demonstrates Rodin's versatility is a playbill for *Le Repas du Lion* reproducing the drawing of a man with a snake coiled around his body, reminiscent of the Baudelaire illustrations.

1. Riotor, *Auguste Rodin, Statuaire*, 25.

I. Octave Mirbeau. *Sébastien Roch*. 1892.
Frontispiece: facsimile of pen and ink portrait of Octave Mirbeau, profile and front view on same sheet; drawing coped from the sculpture bust of 1889 (reproduced in Grappe, no. 230).
References: Edmond de Goncourt, "Le Grenier," *Gazette des Beaux-Arts*, March 1896, 191; *La Plume*, special issue devoted to Rodin, 1900, 79.

167   Frontispiece for *Sébastien Roch* by Octave Mirbeau, 1892. Facsimile of pen and ink drawing. Location and dimensions unknown. Reproduced from *La Plume*, special issue devoted to Rodin, 1900, 79.

II. Gustave Geffroy. *La Vie artistique*. Deuxième série. Paris: E. Dentu, 1893.
Frontispiece: original drypoint *Souls of Purgatory* (see drypoint no. XII, Fig. 69).

III. François de Curel. *Le Repas du Lion*.
Playbill, November 26, 1897.
Illustration: facsimile of a Rodin drawing depicting a nude male figure with a serpent coiled around his body, c. 1880–1885.
Reference: *The Avant-garde in Theatre and Art: French Playbills of the 1890's*, essay by Daryl R. Rubenstein, introduction by Alan M. Fern, an exhibition circulated by the Smithsonian Institution Traveling Exhibition Service, June 1972, 28, reproduced no. 64.

167

IV. Octave Mirbeau. *Le Jardin des Supplices.*
Paris: Librairie Charpentier et Fasquelle, 1899.
Frontispiece: drawing by Rodin of a standing nude woman reproduced in color by Auguste Clot.
Edition of 500, numbered copies on *vélin de cuvre* paper.
Coll: Bibliothèque Nationale (copy no. 62).

168   Frontispiece for *Le Jardin des Supplices* by Octave Mirbeau, 1899. Color reproduction of a watercolor drawing by Rodin, printed by Auguste Clot. 9⅝ x 6¼ in. (24.4 x 15.9 cm.) (page size). Bibliothèque Nationale.

V. Léon Riotor. *Auguste Rodin, Statuaire.*
Paris: J. Royer, 1900.
Frontispiece: facsimile of drypoint *The Dying Centaur* (see drypoint no. XI, Fig. 64.)

VI. Victor Hugo. *Cinq Poèmes.*
Paris: E. Pelletan, 1902.
Complete title: "*Cinq Poèmes: Booz Endormi, Bivar, O Soldats de l'An Deux! Après la Bataille, Les Pauvres Gens.*"
Ornés de Trente-cinq compositions de Eugène Carrière, Daniel Vierge, Willette, Dunki, et Steinlen. Gravées par F. et E. Florian, Crosbie, Duplessis, Perrichon, Emile et Eugène Froment. Précédé d'un portrait par A. Rodin. Gravé par L. Perrichon.
Frontispiece: wood engraving by L. Perrichon after Rodin's bust of *Victor Hugo* from the *Monument to Victor Hugo.*
Edition of 225 numbered copies.

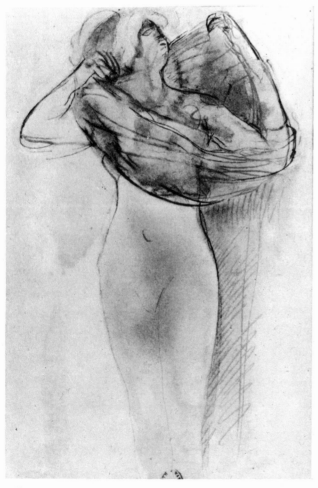

168

Selected Bibliography

Books on Rodin with Citations on
His Drypoints, Lithograph and Illustrations

Bergerat, Emile. *Souvenirs d'un enfant de Paris.* Vol. 3. Paris: E. Fasquelle, 1911–1912.

Cladel, Judith. *Auguste Rodin pris sur la vie.* Paris: Editions de La Plume, 1903.

——. *Auguste Rodin, l'œuvre et l'homme.* Brussels: Van Oest, 1908.

——. *Rodin: The Man and His Art.* New York: The Century Co., 1917.

——. *Rodin.* Translated by James Whitall. New York: Harcourt, Brace & Co., 1937.

Elsen, Albert (ed.). *Auguste Rodin, Readings on His Life and Work.* Englewood Cliffs, N.J.: Prentice Hall, 1965.

——. *Rodin.* New York: The Museum of Modern Art, 1963.

——. *Rodin's Gates of Hell.* Minneapolis: University of Minnesota Press, 1960.

Elsen, Albert, and Varnedoe, J. Kirk T. *The Drawings of Rodin.* With additional contributions by Elisabeth Chase Geissbuhler and Victoria Thorson. New York: Praeger, 1971.

Goncourt, Edmond de. *Journal des Goncourt.* Vol. 7. Paris: Bibliothèque Charpentier, 1894.

Grappe, Georges. *Catalogue du Musée Rodin.* Paris: Editions of 1929, 1931, 1934, 1938, 1944.

Gsell, Paul. *Art by Auguste Rodin.* Boston: Small, Maynard & Co., 1912.

Lawton, Frederick. *The Life and Work of Auguste Rodin.* New York: Charles Scribner's Sons, 1907.

Thorson, Victoria. *The Late Drawings of Auguste Rodin.* Ph.D. Dissertation for The University of Michigan, Ann Arbor, 1973.

Varnedoe, J. Kirk T. *Chronology and Authenticity in the Drawings of Auguste Rodin.* Ph.D. Dissertation for Stanford University, 1972.

References for the Drypoints and Lithograph

Bénédite, Léonce. "Propos sur Rodin," *L'Art et les Artistes,* 1, 1905, 27–32. Same article in *L'Art et les Artistes,* special issue devoted to Rodin, 1914, 85–90.

Catalogue des Estampes Modernes Composant la Collection Loys Delteil. Hôtel Druout, June 13–15, 1928.

Catalogue des Estampes Modernes Composant la Collection Roger Marx. Hôtel Druout, expert Loys Delteil, May 2, 1914.

Delteil, Loys. *Rude, Barye, Carpeaux, Rodin—Le Peintre-graveur illustré XIX et XX siècles.* Vol. 6. Paris: Delteil, 1910.

Elsen, Albert. "Rodin's 'La Ronde,'" *Burlington Magazine,* 107, no. 747, June 1965, 290–99.

Geffroy, Gustave. *La Vie artistique.* Deuxième série. Paris: E. Dentu, 1893.

——. *Le Statuaire Rodin.* Paris: Boussod, Valadon et Cie., 1889. Same article in *Les Lettres et les Arts,* September, 1889, 289–304.

Grautoff, Otto. *Rodin.* Vielefeld und Leipzig: Verlag von Belhagen & Klasing, 1911.

La Revue des Beaux-Arts et des Lettres, special issue devoted to Rodin, January 1, 1899.

L'Art et les Artistes, 1, June 1905, opp. 2.

L'Artiste, February 1885, opp. 156.

Les Maîtres Artistes, special issue devoted to Rodin, October 15, 1903.

L'Estampe originale. Preface by Roger Marx. Paris: Edition du "Journal des Artistes," 1893, *première année.*

Maillard, Léon. *Auguste Rodin, Statuaire.* Paris: H. Floury, 1899.

Marx, Roger. "Auguste Rodin," *Pan,* 3, no. 3, 1897, 191–196.

——. *Auguste Rodin, Céramiste.* Paris: Société de la propagation des livres d'art, 1907.

——. *Les Pointes Sèches de Rodin.* Paris: Gazette des Beaux-Arts, 1902. Same article in *Gazette des Beaux-Arts,* 27, no. 1, March 1902, 204–208.

——. *Maîtres d'Hier et d'Aujourd'hui.* Paris: Calmann–Levy, 1914.

——. "Rodin et Legros," *Le Figaro,* June 1, 1900.

Musée Rodin Archives. Letters to Rodin from Loys Delteil, Alphonse Legros, Roger Marx and Antonin Proust.

Riotor, Léon. *Auguste Rodin, Statuaire.* Paris: J. Royer, 1900.

Roger-Marx, Claude, "Engravings by Sculptors in France," *Print Collectors Quarterly,* 16, no. 2, April 1929, 145–64.

——. *Graphic Art of the 19th Century.* London: Thames and Hudson, 1962.

——. "Rodin Ressenateur et Graveur," *Arts et Métiers Graphiques,* 25, September 1931, 349–355.

Sparrow, Shaw. "Auguste Rodin's Dry-Point Engravings," *The Studio,* 28, March 1903, 88–93.

Stein, Donna M. *L'Estampe originale, A Catalogue Raisonné.* New York: The Museum of Graphic Arts, 1970.

Staatliche Museum of Berlin, Drawings and Prints Department Archives. Letter from Rodin to M. Bourcard, March 25, 1903.

Une Collection Merveilleuse des Eaux-Fortes, Lithographies et Clichés-Verres des Grands Maîtres Français du XIX siècle. H. Gilhofer and H. Ranschburg Ltd., Lucerne, Vente aux Enchères à Lucerne, June 8–9, 1926, 36.

References for the Illustrations

Delteil, Loys. *Rude, Barye, Carpeaux, Rodin—Le Peintre-graveur illustré XIX et XX siècles.* Vol. 6. Paris: Delteil, 1910.

Fague, Felicien. "Ses Collaborateurs," *La Revue des Beaux-Arts et des Lettres*, special issue devoted to Rodin, January 1, 1899, 13.

Grappe, Georges. "Ovide et Rodin," *L'Amour de l'Art*, June 1936, 203–208.

Groschwitz, T. F. Gustave von. "The Significance of XIX Century Color Lithography," *Gazette des Beaux-Arts*, November, 1954, 259–260.

Hofer, Philip. *The Artist and the Book, 1860–1960, in Western Europe and the United States.* Cambridge: Harvard College Library, Department of Printing & Graphic Arts, 1961.

Johnson, Una. *Ambroise Vollard Editeur 1867–1939.* New York: Wittenborn & Co., 1944.

Mahé, Raymond. *Bibliographie des livres de luxe de 1900 à 1928*, Vol. 2. Paris: R. Kieffer, 1931.

Musée Rodin Archives. Letters to Rodin from Emile Bergerat, Auguste Clot, Octave Mirbeau and Ambroise Vollard.

Vollard, Ambroise. *Catalogue complet des éditions Ambroise Vollard*, Le Portique, Paris, December 15, 1930–January 15, 1931.

Albums Reproducing Rodin Drawings During His Lifetime

Album des peintres-graveurs. Collection of lithographs with one Rodin drawing lithographed by A. Clot. Paris: Ambroise Vollard, 1897.

Dix Dessins Choisis. Ten Rodin drawings reproduced by the colored etchings of H. Boutet. Paris: Au Depens de l'Artiste, 1904.

Germinal. Collection of lithographs with one Rodin drawing lithographed by A. Clot. Paris: La Maison Moderne, 1899.

L'Epreuve. A monthly periodical issued as an album with one Rodin drawing reproduced by the wood engraving of A. Lepère, December 1894 to November 1895.

Les Dessins d'Auguste Rodin. Preface by Octave Mirbeau. Collection of Rodin drawings reproduced by photogravure. Paris: Boussod, Manzi, Joyant, & Cie., 1897.

Literary Works Reproducing Rodin Drawings During His Lifetime

Carr, H. D. *Rosa Cœli.* London: Chiswick Press, 1907.

——. *Rosa Inferni.* London: Chiswick Press, 1907.

——. *Rosa Mundi, A Poem with an Original Composition by Auguste Rodin.* Paris: P. H. Renouard, 1905; and London: H. D. Carr, care of E. Dennes, 1905.

Crowley, Aleichester. *Seven Lithographs by Clot, from the Water-Colours of Auguste Rodin, with a Chaplet of Verse by Aleichester Crowley.* London: Chiswick Press, 1907.

Humilis. *Les Poèmes d'Humilis.* Paris: Collection "La Poètique," 1910.

Appendix A

45

Appendix B

Contract for deluxe edition of *Le Jardin des Supplices*, drawn up between
Rodin, Octave Mirbeau and Ambroise Vollard, dated February 10, 1899.
Musée Rodin archives, Vollard folder.

Entre M. Vollard d'une part et Messrs. Mirbeau et Rodin, d'autre part, il a
été convenu ce qui suit————
M. Mirbeau donne par le present à M. Vollard le droit d'éditer à deux cents
exemplaires son livre "Le Jardin des Supplices" qui sera illustré hors texte
d'une vingtaine environ—ce chiffre est un minimum—de compositions
originales de M. Rodin faites exclusivement pour cette édition. Aucun droit
d'auteur ne sera dû à Messrs. Mirbeau et Rodin, autre que deux exemplaires
du "Jardin des Supplices" pour chacun d'eux. M. Vollard soumettra à M.
Mirbeau les caractères typographiques, et il est convenu que l'impression des
compositions de M. Rodin sera faite par Clot. Messrs. Mirbeau et Rodin
s'engagent à signer de leur paraphe chacun des exemplaires du "Jardin des
Supplices." Fait en trois exemplaires à Paris, le Dix Février 1899————

Lu et apprové   Lu et apprové
Octave Mirbeau   Vollard
[left margin postscript]
Les compositions du M. Rodin seront en couleurs. Il sera donné quatre
exemplaires au lieu du deux à Messrs. Mirbeau et Rodin. Il sera donné un
exemplaire au British Museum et au Musée de [Dresden?] s'il ne soucrit
pas. / Vollard / Une exemplaire aussi pour l'amérique / Vollard / Lu et
approuvé la remarque / Octave Mirbeau.

W